PREFACE.

> ... "to know
> That which before us lies in daily life
> Is the prime wisdom. What is more is fume,
> Or emptiness, or fond impertinence,
> And renders us, in things that most concern,
> Unpractic'd, unprepar'd, and still to seek."
>
> —*Milton's Adam to Angel.*

Experience is honored.

This book is the result of experience.

Man is interested in what pertains to health.

We are positive that the ideas herein set forth are healthful.

Our profession is not that of a doctor of chemical medicines.

We have no hobby to ride or patent panacea to advertise, but desire to express, in plain, forcible, truthful language, the methods by which mankind can practically achieve health, happiness and longevity. These go together. Why should they not? Related, dependent upon each other, the great objects of human life, the culmination of all physical and worldly pleasure are contained in them.

Whether you are the perfect embodiment of a business man or the ideal disciple of a certain profession, you cannot possibly reach the highest or even most lucrative grades of your calling without health, happiness, and their logical consequence, longevity. They will prove trusty lieutenants. Without them the battle of life will draw to a close in retreat and end in defeat.

To assert that the average man can enjoy health without medicine, happiness without even money, and longevity too, is a broad and sweeping declaration. In fact, we expect to have opposition from those who have not tried the formula laid down in the following pages.

To *keep* yourself in health without medicine is what we intend to convey; and we assert that but little or no medicine is necessary to reach that condition. To have happiness without any money (in the present condition of society) is not what we claim, but that more happiness can be extracted from a competency than by more or less.

To live to good old age means with us 80 to 120 years, to increase with future generations, when order, regularity, sobriety, cleanliness, and love for the whole human family, shall be paramount in the political, moral, and intellectual world.

The author is living on thirty years of made land. In other words, according to medical diagnosis, he should have *died* thirty years ago! Hence he desires to put before the unhealthy, unhappy, and short-lived human race the result of his experience of half a century. Having battled with a score of diseases, a number of which were claimed to be absolutely incurable—having freed himself entirely of them all—having been completely restored to health and happiness, he honestly believes that he has a convincing right to be heard.

You can now prove for yourself.

CHAPTER I.

"Health is the vital principle of bliss, And exercise of health."

Health, *Happiness*, and *Longevity*. What a talisman is here! In them is the magic that can rule all men. No seal, figure, character, engraven on a sympathetic stone, can equal their single or combined influence. Say to your fellow-man, "If you follow my direction I will confer upon you health, happiness, and longevity," and you will receive his lasting gratitude. He will always be your friend. Money is potent, but these qualities are, as it were, omnipotent. Money alone cannot bring them; they alone can make wealth.

This work is *not* a *philosophical* treatise, difficult to read and more so to comprehend. Its ideas are simple, the result of long *experience* and *observation*. Its propositions are easily demonstrated. Then, my reader, do not think you are perusing the hobbies of a crank, the fantasies of a dreamer, and the preachings of him who does not practice. The world has been so flooded with worthless productions of such characters that we fear we must combat severe *prejudice*. Will you lay that aside? If so we will not only interest but instruct you. Agreeing with our premises and conclusions, you will certainly reap some benefit; not agreeing, you will be tempted to further investigation, which will inevitably prove the strength of our position.

This book was not written at one sitting or many, but it is the culmination of several *years' preparation*. While the first part is the result of thorough reasoning and experience, the second is a collection of the best modern data on prominent diseases and their remedies, with our own annotations. Both sections represent thoughtful and painstaking labor. Even if you are so bold as to maintain that you possess health, happiness, and are sure of longevity, we believe you cannot fail to find practical, valuable truths in these pages. Whether you are an editor, merchant, lawyer, doctor, minister, or day-laborer, we hope at least to entertain you. Are we right? Read and judge.

From the mythological times of *Æsculapius* down to the present day, votaries of medical science have been compounding, diagnosing, and prescribing for helpless, suffering humanity. For many ages this condition may have been a necessity, but in the light of our present civilization, sound common sense is the best physician. That *doctors* cannot be trusted to be right in every instance or even in a majority of them is shown by practical experiments. They certainly are well proved to be an inharmonious crowd by the experience of a *Boston Globe* reporter, who recently called upon ten regular physicians on the same day, and described his symptoms in exactly the same language to each. He received ten prescriptions, of which no two were alike, and a majority were utterly inconsistent each with the other. *Nellie Bly*, the famous lady writer of the New York *World*, had a cold and went to over fifty of the city's leading physicians, in October, 1889, asking them to prescribe for her. They did, and among the collection there were no two alike, and many diametrically opposite in nature and effect!

In a lecture recently delivered before the Cooper Medical College, San Francisco, Cal., on the subject of "Quacks and Quackery," by Prof. L. C. Lane, the speaker said: "Every good thing in the world has been counterfeited, and in these advanced times the work is so well done that it takes an expert to detect the true from the false. Everything is now more or less adulterated, especially the food we consume. The three great professions also of theology, law, and medicine, have been and are grossly counterfeited, especially the latter, which opens up the widest field for imposture."

As the above quotations, without an explanation, might convey the idea to the reader that the author considers that doctors, dentists, and specialists are no longer a necessity, I will say, Under the present state of society, they are not only indispensable, but absolutely a necessity. When you are ill, and do not know what is the matter with you, or if you know the nature of your ailments, and do not know a remedy, seek a first-class physician; take his advice in every particular until he either cures you or you are convinced he cannot. I am not a prophet, nor the son of one, but I will venture an opinion that before the close of the next century, the position of the minister, teacher, and physician will be filled by one and the same person. The teacher *then* will fill the most exalted position on the earth. He will not only instruct how to navigate the air without collision, but how not to catch cold at 30,000 feet elevation in your shirt sleeves, and *who* and *what* is *God*. His school-house will sit upon the most elevated spot in his district, with light reflected from all four sides; it will be at least fifty feet from the floor of his school-room to the ceiling; and in place of a steeple, there will be a dome, containing a 100-inch refractor telescope, and with the extra timber not used for a *steeple,* the seats will be made more comfortable, and pure filtered water will be supplied for the pupils to drink.

It is granted that the majority of mankind appreciate health, desire happiness, and expect longevity. With this as an incentive, why not strive to win the prize? Do not depend on the doctor, do not think some drug must be applied or imbibed for every ill; there are other methods.

Perhaps we can aid you to the true enjoyment of life if you will *impartially* weigh our *argument.* Here is an *editor* suffering from nervousness. He consults a physician, who hands him an opiate so that he can sleep. Better if he had given up all thought of his paper and battles of words, on leaving his office, and allowed his throbbing, weary brain a deserving rest. Then the cells of this brainy tissue would cease to be gorged with blood, and sleep would positively follow. Again, there is a *clergyman* every Sunday beseeching his flock to obey the commandments of the *Bible*; while every day, through carelessness, he is breaking the laws of health. If an *all-wise Being* gave us our bodies as homes of our souls, did he not mean that we should promote the happiness of the soul by providing for it a healthy residence? What logic and strength exist in a religion that does not countenance such philosophy? The majority of mankind admire a well-developed *physique*. The minister wishes and prays to influence the masses of men. Can he reach them effectively, can he point to himself as an example, can he sway them by any reasoning or eloquence, when he himself has a husky voice, a pallid face, and a weakened figure? Indeed, the cowled, decrepit monk could lead the world in the darkness of the middle ages; but in the brightness of the nineteenth century his scepter is powerless.

Health, Happiness and *Longevity* seem to be all that is required for mortal man. They are the foundation, the superstructure, and the apex respectively of the great *Pyramid* of life. Who would desire more than the possession of perfect health, the realization of happiness, the achievement of ripe old age, retaining all the pleasurable attributes of Perfected Manhood, experiencing all these until called upon to surrender this present house of clay for a more advanced state, whatever that may be? Such degrees of soundness, felicity, and age, which we have mentioned, are within the reach of all who desire them, if they will observe the rules implied in the following terms, arranged in the order of their importance: Regularity, Cleanliness, Temperance (or moderation), Morality, and Self-control. It is safe to state the proposition that there is not one in a thousand of those induced to peruse this humble effort, who will not claim to possess one or more of the foregoing virtues, while a fair minority will urge that they are characterized by all of them.

That your *egoism* may not get the better of you in the start and bias you before reading my talk, I will frankly say that there is hardly a person living to-day who is either regular, cleanly, temperate, moral, or self-controlled. It is a fact that some have made fair efforts in those lines of action, but we shall attempt to prove that not any have perfected themselves in a single attribute above mentioned. With us, regularity, cleanliness, temperance, morality, and self-control are so interlaced as to become synonymous terms, the perfection of any one of which means the consummation of all, while their master could laugh at sorrow, pain, and even death, for through long years they would pass his door and forget to knock. Just in proportion as we approximate these virtues, correspondingly will our *lives* be prolonged and our *happiness* intensified. *Fear* will not prostrate us because

"Death rides on every passing breeze, He lurks in every flower."

As modifying the foregoing partially, let us understand, however, that it is possible to have health and longevity to a wonderful degree without cleanliness, temperance, morality, and self-control, on one vital consideration. That is, the *continual* exercise of *regularity*. Here we have the corner-stone of the whole structure of health, the cardinal first law. But can we be happy without the generous employment of *all* these virtues? Obviously and fortunately, we cannot. *Health* is also the chief *desideratum* to happiness. As disease creeps through the physical frame, as aches and pains increase and torment our bodies, our *doubts* supplant *faith* in the *Source* of all goodness.

After a quarter of a century's constant devotion, in sackcloth and ashes, as it were, attempting to free the body from the shackles of pulmonary consumption, and growing gradually worse during the whole period, the majority of devotees, we think, would begin to inquire, "Are our prayers lacking sincerity? or is the Source of goodness at this time otherwise occupied? or may it not be that this for which I ask, I must seek by personal action?" We will try this self-helping method; if success comes, we will return to the same altar with a more exalted idea of a higher Source. Cleansed of our maladies, we will have a clearer perception of who and what is God.

CHAPTER II.

"There is naught like universal co-operation to promote universal achievement."

Individuals may seek and obtain health through the agencies already, and to be, suggested. To keep in health, their *neighbors* must be induced or compelled to adopt the same course. This is not an absolute law, but manifestly is very essential. Supposing your own house, sidewalk, alley, or yard, are comparatively immaculate, it will be impossible to live without constant danger and exposure if your friend (or enemy in this sense) has an untidy house, a dirty sidewalk, and a filthy yard, in your proximity. Then how encouraging to note that health is as contagious as disease. It even spreads with greater rapidity. Health is gladly welcomed; disease is shunned like a deadly poison. All over the world past and contemporary history proves that, once started, health spreads at a rate that disease cannot follow. What will surely result? Healthful communities will make healthful municipalities; healthful municipalities will end in commonwealths and nations of like character. The whole earth will be leavened. From a record of 34 years as the average *duration* of human life, the thermometer of universal progress will point to the threescore and ten, or 70 years.

If you were induced to smile at the close of the last sentence, it shows that you are not lost to all sense of appreciation—but quietly put on your sober cap for a moment and read a few facts on *vital statistics*. The average length of life up to twenty years ago was 33 years, now it has reached about 34.8 years. This has not been caused by the *whole* world becoming more healthful—indeed, some portions of the earth, including sections of the United States, have retrograded, and the former limit of *mortality* has been lowered—but by the health of a number of *organizations*, *sects*, and individuals who have increased their standards of regularity, cleanliness, temperance, morality, and self-control. Thus the average rate of mortality has been raised nearly 2%. An interesting fact which is new to the majority of persons is this, that the whole sect of *Friends*, or *Quakers*, live an average of 58 years per individual. In the thirty-two years from 1850 to

1882 they raised the average six years, or about one year in five. With this ratio, which is itself increasing, the plurality of Quakers will be centenarians in less than two hundred years—in half that time if assisted by the world at large. By the foregoing it will be seen that the whole organization of Friends live 70% longer than the general age allotted to mankind, which includes them to make up the universal rate. Another noticeable feature in connection with the Quakers' life is this, the deaths among them average 18 in every thousand; in the general population, 22 per thousand; while the amount given to charities per inhabitant in that sect is $7.78, and in the total population the average is $1.46. Why this difference in longevity to so marked a degree?

The *prohibitionist* will give this reason, that the Friends dissipate less; the religionists will say they are more truthful, more godly. While each of the aforementioned reasons have a healthful tendency, there is a more scientific conclusion, for it is a well-known fact that there are thousands of cases of longevity of men and women who lack every moral principle, and dissipate all their lives. The *scientist* comes to our rescue. He tells us that the Quaker's life is prolonged by his methodical way of living, evenness of temperament, wearing the same weight of clothing, allowing nothing to furrow the brow, regularity of sleeping, drinking, exercising, and eating. He takes no food or drink into his stomach above 100° or below 50° Fahr. *Boiling* hot soup and frozen *ice-cream* are unknown in a Quaker family. This might convey the idea that ice-cream is foresworn by them. Not entirely so. They use the same good judgment in that as in every other indulgence, allowing the cream to rise in temperature from 10° to 15° above the freezing point, to soft consistency, before it is taken into the stomach. Dr. Ufflemann, a German physician of authority, draws some important conclusions from his own experiments and those of others. The rules laid down are briefly:—

1. That, in general, a temperature of food which approaches that of the blood is most healthful.

2. For quenching the thirst the best temperature is from 50° Fahr. to 68° Fahr. Americans prefer about 40°.

3. The gulping down of ice-water or hot coffee, etc., means eventually a stomach damnation.

4. The use of very hot and cold substances, following or alternating, is injurious to the teeth.

5. Ingestion of cold food and drinks lessens the bodily temperature, whether it be normal or febrile.

6. Cold food and drinks increase the tendency to cough, by causing, reflexly, a congestion of the bronchial vessels. Hence persons with bronchial disease ought not to indulge in cold drinks.

The habits of indulgence in alcoholic drinks, tobacco, opium, and other narcotics or stimulants, have less to do than is generally supposed with longevity, but much to do with happiness, while their abuse or irregularity determines all for health, happiness, and longevity combined. Temperance men and moralists will take issue with me, and undertake to prove that any quantity, no matter how small, of either alcohol, tobacco, or opium will shorten life; but the facts will not sustain the assertion. It is the irregularity with which the body is treated, either by outward application or bathing, in eating, sleeping, or excess in all vices. For health, a regular gratification in the full list of vices is better than having no vices—such as are so termed by the world—and being irregular in everything else. While I do not believe in practising any form of vice, yet the man who takes six drinks of alcoholic spirits in reasonable quantities at fixed intervals each day, smokes six cigars—two after each meal—chews three ounces of tobacco with the same punctuality every day, eats his meals slowly and at stated periods, sleeps from 8-1/2 to 9 hours per night between the same hours, will outlive the man who neither smokes, chews, or drinks, but does eat and sleep irregularly, and lies awake all night hating his neighbor for his immoralities. He gets thin and haggard, followed by all the weaknesses to which his system is heir; while the other man, with his evenness of nature, habits, and dissipations, enjoys health, becomes fat, and lives to the proverbial good old age.

Here, then, my reader, we have the explanation why a man may live through *dissipation* all his life, and then die only by accident at 80 or 100 years of age. A beggar, miser, or hermit may by degrees contract the habit of filthiness, non-bathing, scantiness of food and improper clothing, with such regularity that he will outlive all his friends and relatives, and be chronicled at his death as one of the *centenarians*. As an interesting fact, we state that in 1888 a beggar, aged 84, in Perth, Hungary, tried to commit suicide by throwing himself into the Danube because he was no longer able to support his father and mother, who were 115 and 110 years old respectively! *Poisons* may be taken in infinitesimal doses for a while, then increasing by degrees until *twenty* grains of morphia or strychnia may be taken at a single dose without immediate injury. There is at least one case of positive record in Colusa County, of this State.

In closing this chapter we wish to call attention to a reasonable result of true system, or regularity. Here is a *convict* in the State prison. Before he was incarcerated his health was imperfect, and he wore a sallow, dejected look; but behold him after six months of strict penitentiary discipline; he is a well man, fat and sleek—no longer a semi-invalid. There are exceptions, but they are due to melancholy generally. A *soldier* after he enlists, unless he is exposed to the constant privations of protracted war, throws off most defects in his physique. You must know the cause; it is the compulsory regulation of diet and clothing. Cleanliness and regularity are forced upon them, showing it to be just what they needed.

CHAPTER III.

"Let health my nerves and finer fibers brace."

The possession of health, happiness, and longevity requires *not* so much a general literary and *scientific education*, as a *practical knowledge* of one's own self. The latter will far outweigh the other. In many ways, however, will these qualities be improved by the former. A person must know what is regularity, cleanliness, and temperance, or moderation. By the use of these effective auxiliaries, I have freed myself of so many maladies within the last thirty years that the average medical devotee will laugh in derision and question my trustworthiness. For the first *eleven* years of my life I had *seven* years of wasting sickness. Of these, *five* were spent in bed. At the age of 22 I left a clerkship in New York City to come to California, *via* Cape Horn. *Consumption* was strongly seated on my lungs. In addition to this dangerous affliction I had bronchitis, catarrh, constipation, piles, periodical rheumatism, cataracts on my eyes, corns on my feet, and fever and ague from one to three months every year. Surely I was in a position to sympathize with *Job*, but impatient, rather than patient like the Biblical hero. I set myself towards absolute health. Before I had been in this State two years, I gained the mastery of the lung and throat troubles; but while assisting in putting in a flume in Feather River, below Oroville, in 1859, I ruptured myself so that for twenty-five years I wore a truss. Now I am entirely rid of the aforementioned list of ailments, including hernia.

The detail of how I treated each of the maladies might not interest the reader, and is too long a story to relate in this work. The principal things done in each case, however, will be chronicled under their proper heads in the second part of this work. See index. I do not now smoke, chew, nor drink intoxicants; the latter I did to a limited degree, and the former to excess, for a number of years, up to the close of 1869. On the 31st day of December of that year—the day I smoked my *last cigar*—I bought *twenty-five* cigars and smoked *twenty-three* of them. My cigar bill that year averaged $2.50 per day, and ran as high as $4.00. Having dissipated, and had nearly every form of disease, I speak from my own thorough experience and not from that of anyone else. Why should not my story, then, have a beneficial influence? If any man knows how he can improve the welfare of his fellows, it is his duty to spread the information. True it is that many of the *quasi reformers*, or informers, are cranks or dreamers; but we wish the fact distinctly understood and appreciated that we come not under that category. We raise no false standard; we send forth no untried hypothesis. There is a man in a New England State who annually lectures on agriculture, writes special and general articles for the country papers on the most improved methods of farming, appears before legislative committees as a successful tiller of the soil. But, alas! what superficiality is contained in this man's brain. His house is a barn, his garden a chicken-yard, his orchard a forest, and his meadow a pasture. There are like phantasmagoric geniuses interested in the health question. We simply say, Trust them not. Shun them and their advice as you would the presence and enticings of a bunco steerer. But you will get impatient to learn in what consists cleanliness, regularity, and temperance if I do not proceed. Indeed, I think I can hear some of you say, "I neither chew, drink, smoke, eat irregularly, or miss my stipulated number of hours in bed; yet I have all manner of aches and pains, and many lingering maladies." If such be the case, you do not understand the true principle and its practical application of *cleanliness*. A word here in regard to bathing. There is no doubt we all should bathe at least once a day. It should be done either at retiring or rising. If a warm or hot bath, at night; if cold or sponge bath, in the morning. Of course, if a person is not accustomed to a cold sponge bath, or is quite nervous, he must not attempt it too strongly at first. Commence and advance by gradation. Almost anything can be done to which an individual is unaccustomed if regular steps are taken towards the end, and not one leap. Whether it be beneficial or destructive, invigorating or poisoning, gradation will accomplish the end.

Madame Patti, who always has been obliged to take the greatest care of herself, gives this warning, which may not be out of place: "Take plenty of exercise, take it in the open air, take it alone, and breathe with the mouth closed. Live on simple food; all the fruit and rare beef you want, very little pastry, a glass of claret for dinner, coffee in moderation, but never a sip of beer, because it thickens the voice and stupefies the senses. Keep regular hours for work, meals, rest, and recreation, and never under any circumstances indulge in the fashionable habit of eating late suppers. If you want to preserve the beauty of face, and the priceless beauty of youth, keep well, keep clean, keep erect, and keep cool." Without being didactic, let me detail to you a few things you should and should not do; and all of which I carry out to the letter:—

Adopt some style of *clothing* so that even if you change the color the *weight* will be about the *same*.

Wear no overcoat, overshoes, nor gloves; in their place wear a sufficiently heavy suit when it is warm, so as to have enough on when it is cold. By wearing a *chest protector* fore and aft of the lungs, made of chamois and flannel, over the under-garment and under the shirt, you will never take cold through your lungs.

Have good, thick-soled *boots*—and always of the same thickness—and you will not take cold through your feet.

Have a *hat* always of the same weight, and that should be light, with ventilators in the top or sides. If you do not wear your hat at the lunch table, or in your place of business, you will not catch cold in your head.

A large list of accessories accompany the above:—

Never sit at your desk or home fireside with the same coat which you use on the street. In its place have one 50 per cent lighter for such occasions and positions.

Never *sleep* in your *under-garments*, nor in any other clothing that you carry during the day. The reason is strong and obvious. Your covering in the course of the day receives all the perspiration and surface deposit of the skin, which amounts to considerable in sixteen hours. This must have a chance to escape or be absorbed by the air. The amount is only increased by wearing the same garments at night. Have a good warm *night-shirt*, and a clean one at least every week.

Do not sleep in a room without having the windows down from the top to some extent. If there be six, lower three of them.

If you sleep with a companion and do not know anything about *animal magnetism*, find out through someone who does know. Ascertain which of you is more positive, and govern yourself accordingly. I find best results for me in sleeping with my head north, and on the west side of a negative companion. This principle of magnetism is too little observed. Yet it applies to all persons at all times. Naturally some individuals are more magnetic than others, that is, more positive. Usually, if not always, the more masculine, swarthy, is the more positive, while the light-haired and eyed are negative. Sleep invariably with your head towards the north if you are positive, towards the west if you are negative, but never in any case towards the east or south.

These conclusions are based wholly on scientific reasons, and anyone who understands physics will see the cogency of our statements.

As a preventative against anything that has once been in my stomach rising and remaining on the tongue, I use a piece of ordinary *whalebone* to curry it every morning, from end to end. This will tend to purify the breath, sweeten the mouth, and aid mastication.

My *tooth brush*, after using, is so thoroughly *cleansed* and dried that anyone acquainted with the facts would hardly believe it had been used.

There are millions of particles of dust, atoms, *microbes*, or any other name you may use, that collect upon your person and clothing hourly. If your garments be tattered and torn, or patched and glazed, this will not shorten your life or lessen your appetite; but I assure you, if you will use up a 15-cent whisk-broom twice a year, in brushing yourself from head to foot before each meal, there will be less to fall upon your food, and thus find its way to your stomach, and your days will be prolonged in exact ratio.

CHAPTER IV.

"On life's vast ocean diversely we sail, Reason the card, but passion is the gale."

There are more diseases contracted, more unhappiness created during life, and early decay occasioned, by *politeness* and *pride* than by whisky and tobacco combined. Total-abstinence advocates will assert that drink kills more than all other causes. What would they think if we should say, if he is a reformed drinker, that it was out of pure politeness that he quaffed his first glass.

Politeness is the cause of disease in many ways, of which the following are a few:—

A friend—only in name—will stop you in the first corner of the street and insist on telling you a good(?) joke about Brown, Smith, or Jones. He takes you by the lapels of the coat, holds you to windward for twenty minutes in a breeze blowing twenty-five miles an hour, although this lays you up with a cold for a week, and thus plants the first seeds of consumption. You will be too polite to tell him that your health will not permit you to be so exposed. As a remedy for this class of attacks, if a man insists on saying anything more than "How do you do" or "Good-bye," I should invite him into the nearest hall-way or around the corner to leeward, entirely out of the draft. If this does not seem feasible, I would bid him "Good-day."

Another case of excessive politeness is when a gentleman or lady continues chatting ten minutes in the *hall* after he or she *must go immediately*. Then at the door after they have walked out, you, in dressing-gown and slippers, stand on the cold marble step in a driving fog for twenty minutes more, to hear the latest gossip—too polite to slam the door in their faces, or excuse it as an accident.

But the politeness that kills faster than any other is that of the consumptive, bronchially-affected, or catarrhal patient. He will sit at the table, or in company, and, out of pure politeness, swallow the *mucus* and other impurities that arise in his throat—too polite to use a cuspidor or excuse himself by withdrawing to another room or the open air, and clear his throat. A great many people are accustomed to *expectorate* into their *handkerchiefs*. This is a baneful practice. Just as soon as that gets dry which they have thrown up from their lungs, innumerable microbes of deadly effect escape and do extensive harm. Avoid this habit and use the cuspidor or step out-of-doors. It is not unreasonable to believe that 50 per cent of all the consumptives would recover if they would, by care and cleanliness, see that no particle of mucus once away from the lungs should ever go back down the throat, and observe other points regarding apparel and cleanliness mentioned in the first part of this work.

We have already devoted some space to what we should and should not do. All that, however, is but a small part of a life which will continually experience health, happiness, and longevity. We trust you do not simply read these statements not intending to test their value. It is not unlikely that many of you from your course or line of business will find it eminently difficult to absolutely follow our instructions. Be that as it may, come as approximately as you can, and there will positively result an improvement in your physical condition, a progression in your happiness, and a realization of longevity. The remainder of this chapter will be occupied by a program, or rather set of *formula* of what is necessary to aid you in *keeping well*, living long and happily.

Keep your *bowels* open and regular in action. This you can do, if irregular or *constipated*, by taking a few drops of water in your right hand every morning and rubbing the bowels in a circular motion from right to left, until a friction is produced and the moisture gone. From six to ten separate passages of the hand over the bowels is usually sufficient, and the object will be accomplished. Each day this is repeated; in a very short time you will be all right in this particular, and will not require even this effective medicine. You must be aware that a score of maladies are kept at bay by the regularity of the bowels. This fact cannot be too strongly impressed on mankind in general. It is very seldom indeed that you come upon a man who is well with a bad digestive apparatus; but, again, he who possesses a strong stomach and is moderate and regular in eating is almost invariably characterized with a vigorous constitution. Disease finds no place to locate upon or in him. There is no doubt the American people eat too fast, and that is why so many die so soon. The system is worn out when it should be ready to do its best work. If all the men and women in this country would eat 50% slower they would live 25% longer. Of this we have no doubt—nor do you, reader.

Sleep eight hours every night, between the same hours, as nearly as possible, in a room well ventilated from the top of the window. If your room is small you will require more *ventilation* than if it is large; in this case use more clothing on the bed. If possible have a bowl or basin of water uncovered in the room, but the next morning do not either drink or wash your face in the water that has stood exposed all night. To drink it is slow suicide; to wash in it is unhealthy.

In the morning scrape the tongue with a strip of whalebone, as before mentioned; brush the teeth with a good stiff clean tooth-brush, up and down, but not across; note this latter proposition, there is reason for it. By perpendicular brushing the bristles or hairs get in between the teeth, where much sediment is left, and the gums are not made sore. This is the best method also to prevent tartar forming. *Gargle* the throat with clean water three or four times; then, if you have it at hand, drink about three swallows of cool filtered water; if not near go thirsty until it is. Never take a drink of water, whether you be sick or well, without first gargling the throat with at least one swallow and spitting it out. Do you think *filtering* of reservoir or general city water is necessary? If not, then make a microscopic examination, and any skepticism will be entirely removed. It is a prominent fact in science to-day that almost all diseases and troubles are started or promulgated by microbes and bacilli. There are often enough of these in one swallow of water to poison a whole family. Then take a moist towel and apply it to every part of your body; follow this with a vigorous rubbing with a dry towel. A sponge bath is recommended by many physicians. This is all right for the first time, but from that on the sponge begins to get foul, not from necessity, but because not one person in fifty will wash and thoroughly *dry* the *sponge*. In any other case it is a disease breeder. Perforated with so many cells and passages, intricate and numberless, it is not surprising that it should be the residence of much that is dangerous.

During the time of your bath you should close the windows of your room to exclude the cold draughts—in any part of the country where the atmosphere moves over two miles per hour—but not the sun. After this lower or raise your window to the height or level of the eyes, and proceed to enjoy a breathing exercise. This is done by first exhausting all the air from the lungs through the mouth, then inhale, slowly, through the nasal organs to the full capacity of the lungs. Do this *three* times or more each morning. If your lungs are not too weak, tap with your fingers on your chest while it is inflated. This will tend to develop your capacity of breathing wonderfully. The gentle percussion thus effected is quite exhilarating. Practice yourself also in *holding* your *breath* for a prolonged interval, but always draw in air through your nostrils; they strain out all impurities.

You are now ready for your breakfast; but, perhaps you say, I am a workingman and have not the time. To such I would reply: I go through all these duties in *one* hour's time, and if belated I accomplish it in *forty minutes*. If I have to take a train at 5 A. M., I see that I am called at 4 A. M., at least, and enjoy my regular time for *toilet*. I would advise those of you who think you have not time, to go to bed that much earlier. Even if you are to travel, by using my method of preparation you will not experience that tired, disagreeable, restless feeling that will otherwise come. You all know how intensely that feeling acts to destroy all your pleasure until the day is half over and it is worn away. Employ common-sense ways and you will be as fresh at 6 as at 12 o'clock. Your lips will not be blue, your skin cold, your teeth unclean, your mouth dry, your eyes red, and your whole self out of sorts as it were.

CHAPTER V.

"Of right choice food are his meals, I ween."

Now as to what you should eat, what you should not eat, and how you should eat. This is perhaps the greatest problem for a man to solve. A man with a bad digestive apparatus is practically an invalid. We have no hesitation in saying that there is as much bodily injury done by over and careless eating among people commonly called temperate as among those who drink alcoholic liquors to a large extent. If you would preserve your vital strength and capabilities for a happy, long period, mind your diet. Don't rest too much on the insane idea that you have a *stomach* of *iron* and that you can digest shingle nails. You are not a species of the genus ostrich, or goat. Then if you really do possess organs that can take care of all kinds of food, their splendid power should not be destroyed or even weakened by improper indulgence. The mightiest engine is soon as valueless as old iron if it is continually exerted to its greatest velocity. If inanimate mechanism cannot stand a permanent strain surely bodily flesh would be quickly disabled.

Some foods are particularly muscle formers, others produce fat, and still others brain and nerve, while most of the common articles of diet combine these uses in varying degrees.

But the question to cover our entire physical needs requires to be broadened into this: What combination of food will best nourish the body? Even then the answer must be modified to suit individual cases, for the digestive power differs greatly in different persons. Moreover, there is an interdependence between the different bodily organs and tissues, so that the body must be built up as a whole. If one part lacks the whole suffers, and if one part is overfed the others will be underfed.

Thus a person who becomes unduly fat loses in muscular fiber, either in quantity or quality. One who overfeeds the brain loses in muscular strength. So, too, muscular development may be carried to such excess as to impoverish the brain, and also to reduce the fat of the body below what is necessary both as surplus food laid up for emergencies, and as a protection against sudden changes of temperature.

The best food for producing muscle, therefore, must, while being duly appetizing, contain a large per cent of nitrates for the muscles, of phosphates for the brain and nerves, and of carbonates for the fat.

Of nitrates, beans stand at 24 per cent, then peas at 22, cabbage and salmon at 20, oats at 17, eggs and veal at 16, and beef at 15.

Of phosphates, salmon stands first at 7, then codfish at 6, beef and eggs at 5, beans and veal at 4, and cabbage, peas, and oats at 3.

Of carbonates, butter stands at the head at 100, rice at 80, corn and rye at 72, wheat at 69, oats at 66, peas at 60, beans at 57, and cabbage at 46.

Fresh codfish fried in fat or served with butter gravy about equals beef in all respects, and so do eggs fried in fat. But we must add:—

The mere eating of food cannot make muscle. The muscles must be called into vigorous daily exercise, yet without overdoing.

Excessive eating is weakening, and must be avoided. It is the amount digested and assimilated that tells, not the quantity taken into the stomach.

All the laws of health must be steadily observed. We are in favor of a diet that excludes meat entirely; and once a day should be the excess of those who indulge in the flesh-eating luxury. A suspicion that there is a difference between merely getting food down into the stomach and its digestion, is abroad, and that a peach, an orange, an apple, a spoonful of flour, or something similar, which is digested, is really better for a man than a beefsteak, which simply passes through the alimentary canal. See "Food" for further consideration of vegetarianism.

For *breakfast* have any of the numerous preparations of *mush*, such as oatmeal, cracked wheat, and germea, every other day some kind of fish; of the miscellaneous, potatoes baked or boiled, eggs poached, boiled, or omelette, and natural fruit; of drinks, water, filtered or boiled, and not below 56° Fahr., milk, pure and sweet but not cream, cocoa, chocolate, tea, or coffee. These are good and beneficial in the order they are placed. The following from the N. Y. *Medical Record* is invaluable information:—

"STIMULANTS (drink most healthful).—Milk heated to much above 100 degrees Fahrenheit loses for a time a degree of its sweetness and density. No one who, fatigued by over-exertion of body or mind, has ever experienced the reviving influence of a tumbler of this beverage, heated as warm as it can be sipped, will willingly forego a resort to it because of its being rendered somewhat less acceptable to the palate. The promptness with which its cordial influence is felt is indeed surprising. Some portion of it seems to be digested and appropriated almost immediately, and many who now fancy they need alcoholic stimulants when exhausted by fatigue will find in this simple draught an equivalent that will be abundantly satisfying and far more enduring in its effects. There is many an ignorant overworked woman who fancies she could not keep up without her beer; she mistakes its momentary exhilaration for strength, and applies the whip instead of nourishment to her poor, exhausted frame. Any honest, intelligent physician will tell her that there is more real strength and nourishment in a slice of bread than in a quart of beer; but if she loves stimulants it would be a very useless piece of information. It is claimed that some of the lady clerks in our own city, and those too who are employed in respectable business houses, are in the habit of ordering ale or beer at the restaurants. They probably claim that they are 'tired,' and no one who sees their faithful devotion to customers all day will doubt their assertions. But they should not mistake beer for a blessing or stimulus for strength. A careful examination of statistics will prove that men and women who do not drink can endure more hardships, and do more work, and live longer, than those less temperate."

If you must eat meat for breakfast, have your *steak rare*, mutton chops well done; if fish, always well done; and if each are fried, use butter, not lard—the same applies to everything else that has to be fried. All meats are sweeter and more healthful broiled than fried. Of bread, for health, natural *graham* comes first; and, in order of nutrition, corn, corn and wheat mixed, rye, and wheat. They should be taken cold and at least twenty-four hours after baking. If the midday meal is a lunch, all dishes should be cold. It can be made up largely from dishes left over from the morning meal, such as cold cracked wheat with milk, natural fruit; add nuts, sauces, jellies, and prepared fruit.

If *dinner* is taken at noon instead of lunch at that hour, any one of the score of vegetable soups are first in value; all other kinds are secondary; let there be from three to six kinds of vegetables cooked; any of the drinks mentioned for breakfast may be used, but none of them iced; cold bread, and no pastry unless an open pie with unshortened undercrust. An excellent morsel for *dyspeptics* is *sea biscuit* dipped in cold water and then placed in a hot oven from three to five minutes. If meat is to be a portion of this meal, you can have beef, mutton, or venison, roasted or broiled, the former rare, and the two latter well done. Provided dinner is enjoyed at the close of the day, it should occur before 5:30 P. M.; if at midday, then the lunch meal can be renamed supper, and can be partaken of as late as 6 or 7 P. M. Let there be no eating two meals for Sundays and holidays, and three for other days, or indulging in them at later hours in the morning and earlier in the evening; for this irregularity will detriment more than many kinds of improper food.

Do not eat *fresh pork*, for this and every other kind of swine flesh is an abomination. Eat no *kidney, liver,* or *tripe*; deal sparingly with *fowl* and all the bird family. Outside impure water and uncleanliness, there can be but one cause for *skin diseases*, eczema, boils, and the dread leprosy, which is the eating of pork, kidney, liver, duck, etc. If the lion indiscriminately kills and eats all kinds of flesh, and thereby is made ferocious, if the lamb is rendered passive and inoffensive by grasses and grains, then what the swine or different domestic fowls eat must have something to do with the make-up of the flesh of their bodies. The hog is the most filthy animal of that nature, while chicken and duck are the most so in the line of fowls used by man for food. It is offensive but true that they will not only *eat* but relish both their own and man's *excrement*.

We cannot use space foolishly, if we show plainly why pork should be abandoned. Did you ever stop to think on what most *swine* live? *Swill* is the most common term for it. Anything and everything that is the refuse of a boarding-house will they eagerly devour. Give them *rotten* apples and potatoes, full of innumerable microbes, and they will relish the repast. Place them in a dung heap—they will root, and eat much of what they find. Now all meat, all flesh and tissue, is made from what an animal or person eats—

if he doesn't eat he grows thin and starves. Then the hog's flesh is made from elements derived from swill, decayed substances, and everything either cooked, uncooked, or even digested, that man is through with or has cast off. You who eat pork relish that which once you have refused to eat—only in another form. Can you enjoy this meat when you consider all this? Surely its use means bad health and contamination. Skin diseases and *poor complexions* are found almost entirely among those who live on these improper foods. Again, even if you feed swine on clean corn, milk, and water, we ascertain by careful experiment and examination that pork is most susceptible to bacteria of almost any meat. Better boycott it altogether. *Leprosy* and skin troubles are found largely among pork-eating people—such as the inhabitants of the Hawaiian Islands, where there are 749 lepers. On the other hand, Jews, who everywhere are marked with clear skins, avoid pork. In Constantinople there are 250 lepers, in Crete upwards of 3,000, and quantities in the islands of eastern Mediterranean Sea, and 1,000 in Norway. These places are all characterized by the great amount of pork, and duck too, that they consume.

Other things not good for *invalids*, and will make strong persons invalids, are: Fried potatoes, hot cakes, warm bread, pound cake, green cucumbers, and rich pie-crust. Eat only those things that will excite the salivary glands to assist digestion. The walls, not the center of the alimentary canal, need attention.

Have your *soup cool* enough so that it will not cause tears in your eyes when you swallow—same with your coffee, tea, and other warm drinks; take no *ice drinks*; if you are used to having water only with your meals, drink it warm with sugar and milk, and *not hot.* If you are obliged to live in a second-class boarding-house or restaurant, and are obliged to take one of three meals each day at such a place, insist on having a *napkin.* Use it first to wipe your glass for water, then follow by polishing every utensil set before you for use at your meal. If note is taken of the napkin before and after each meal, you will be able by a mathematical calculation to tell just how much *real estate* did not belong to you.

How you should eat: Begin with one swallow of cool water. Eat slowly; take full 20 minutes for a hurried meal, and 45 minutes when you have the time. If you eat beefsteak, have it rare; if mutton chops, have them well done; if *fish*, well done and brown; if potatoes, first choice, baked; second, boiled; third, stewed or mashed. Never eat decayed vegetables or fruit; have them fresh or do without them. At table, see that the conversation is pleasant and mirthful. Should any of the younger members of the family insist, at each meal, in changing this order of things, cause them for a short season to sit at a separate table in the kitchen, until this sort of disease—for disease it is—may be cured. Nothing retards digestion, brings dyspepsia, or creates neuralgia, to such extent as a sullen disposition. We will end this chapter with a remarkably bright paraphrase on the ten commandments, which we recently ran across:—

THE TEN HEALTH COMMANDMENTS.

"1. Thou shalt have no other food than at meal-time.

"2. Thou shalt not make unto thee any pies, or put into pastry the likeness of anything that is in the heavens above or in the waters under the earth. Thou shalt not fall to eating it or trying to digest it. For the dyspepsia will be visited upon the children to the third and fourth generation of them that eat pie; and long life and vigor upon those that live prudently and keep the laws of health.

"3. Remember thy bread to bake it well; for he will not be kept sound that eateth his bread as dough.

"4. Thou shalt not indulge sorrow or borrow anxiety in vain.

"5. Six days shalt thou wash and keep thyself clean, and the seventh thou shalt take a great bath; thou, and thy son, and thy daughter, and thy man-servant, and thy maid-servant, and the stranger that is within thy gates. For in six days man sweats and gathers filth and bacteria enough for disease; wherefore the Lord has blessed the bath-tub and hallowed it.

"6. Remember thy sitting-room and bed-chamber to keep them ventilated, that thy days may be long in the land which the Lord thy God giveth thee.

"7. Thou shalt not eat hot biscuit.

"8. Thou shalt not eat thy meat fried.

"9. Thou shalt not swallow thy food unchewed, or highly spiced, or just before hard work, or just after it.

"10. Thou shalt not keep late hours in thy neighbor's house, nor with thy neighbor's wife, nor his man-servant, nor his maid-servant, nor his cards, nor his glass, nor with anything that is thy neighbor's."—*New England Farmer.*

With the use of the foregoing as a guide, and ordinary judgment in the affairs with your fellow-men, life will run smoothly, happiness will follow, and a long life be the result.

CHAPTER VI.

"Let the jewel of happiness poise in the setting of health."

If you are a reader of this work to find out a cure for consumption, catarrh, bronchitis, constipation, hemorrhoids or piles, hernia or rupture, rheumatism, fever and ague, cataracts on the eyes, warts on the hands, corns on the feet, and how to abstain from drink and tobacco in all injurious forms, we will try and not disappoint you. Under the head of each disease above named, see index and second part. We offer you a remedy. All of these troubles I have had (and a score not mentioned), of the entire list of which *I* am now *free completely*. In short, the whole number of diseases that beset the human family can be cured by care, cleanliness, regularity, fresh air, cold water used internally, and by compress, proper clothing, right food, regular exercise, an even disposition, a clear conscience, intelligent and agreeable associates, and a reasonable amount of time.

It took me 30 years, 25 of which I spent ascertaining the way. If someone could have informed me, as this book does you, I would have enjoyed full health *twenty-five* years earlier than I did. Anyone observing the rules I have recounted can restore a broken-down *constitution* in less than 5 years —yes, even if one foot is already in the grave! Soon you will begin to lift it out, and it will be a long period before you will take that step again. I do not exaggerate when I state that I had *both feet* in the grave. Fortunately, however, my head was above-ground, and I began to reason how to get the rest of myself away. The secret was discovered, the causes set to work, and finally the end achieved. To use another figure, my coffin had many nails already driven in it when I secured a clincher, pulled them all out, and then split up the old wooden hulk to make fires with which to start the steam of my new energies.

All of my *time* is *employed*. I do some sort of laborious work every day to start my blood coursing vigorously, and open the pores of my skin. By a proper adjustment of my under-clothing, I prevent a cold, and am always ready with a good appetite when meal-time comes. I have never studied

Anatomy, *Medicine*, or *Surgery*, know but little about the niceties of the English language, but I have studied the Materia Medica of myself, and am aware of just what is beneficial and what is injurious for me.

There is a duty each individual owes to his fellow-man, each municipal corporation to its citizens, and each State and general government to those over whom they preside. Every individual should strive to see how much distress he can relieve during his short stay on this earth; how few thorns he has to place in the pathway of others, and how many drops of oil he can pour on the disturbed waters of the ocean of life.

Accidents that are *preventable*, caused by carelessness, laziness, and ignorance, cost more money, suffering, and life than viciousness and incendiarism, in the ratio of 3 to 1. Every man who builds a mill, manufactory, or a business block, makes his own rate of insurance.

A slight variation in the construction of a building, the omission of certain details, the wrong location of hazardous machinery or materials, or the neglect of cleanliness and order, may very seriously affect the *fire hazard*, and consequently the *rate* of insurance which must necessarily attach to the property.

The *Fire Losses* in the United States amount to $125,000,000 per annum, and the great mass of this enormous loss is chargeable to bad construction of buildings, the lack of necessary apparatus for extinguishing fires, and carelessness in the management of property. The *unavoidable* losses are few in number; the *avoidable*, many. Insurance companies *restore no value, repair no loss*; they can only *distribute* the loss throughout the community. Careless, ignorant, annihilative, is the term to be applied to 75% of the fire losses. The destruction of life by accidents, where immediate death follows, in the United States is large; but, in comparison with those that assist in shortening life, they are about in the ratio of 1 to 100. Only such persons as have undoubted *integrity*, coupled with order, cleanliness, and carefulness should be allowed to insure their property, and this should be restricted by law. A certain sect in our population that now have to be charged from 50 to 100% more for insurance than other people, should be stricken from the list of the insured, until they have by personal action abolished this difference in risk.

When the time comes that only such persons as attend to all the details of cleanliness and prevention of the loss of property and health can be insured, the cost will be reduced 50%. Until we are willing, or educated up to that point, to protect our neighbors' lives and property as if they were ours, we must expect to pay this 50% more for everything we have, use, drink, eat, and wear. Longevity will be restricted in the same proportion. Hundreds of accidents would be prevented by proper care. Throwing foolishly the match, cigar, cigarette, etc., any and everywhere, causes great loss of property, and often life; the unthinking eat oranges and *bananas* in the *street* and cast underfoot the rinds and skins to cause the next moment the *dislocation* of a limb, or broken skull. Over 500 accidents have occurred in this city alone during the last 5 years, occasioned by some sort of vegetable or fruit refuse lying upon the pavements; fatal results, though not all immediate, happened to 15 persons, and a number were maimed for life. Broken bottles and glass thrown into the street and on the sidewalks bring about at times frightful accidents to both man and beast; and if a correct report could be had from each livery-man and teamster in this regard, it would startle the most inhuman of our race.

The *tax-payer* has a tendency to be selfish when he is really doing himself severe injury. It is a case of reflex action. In passing along a thoroughfare he sees a banana skin lying on the sidewalk. He cannot possibly stop or trouble himself to push it into the gutter. Almost immediately another man comes along, steps on the skin, slips, breaks his leg, and is carried to the hospital. He remains there a month, supported by the city, that is, by money paid by the same tax-payer. In this manner, and other ways, can every man act, both selfishly or unselfishly. If selfish in passing this by, it is sure to come back on him a hundred-fold to the original trouble required. His unselfishness will consist in saving his fellow-men from danger by removing the cause. Indeed, he will be selfish if he casts it off for the sake of decreasing his taxation, but such selfish unselfishness will be gladly excused.

Garbage thrown out of back doors or under neighbors' steps creates contagion, and in time the thoughtless individuals fall a prey to their own carelessness. Three out of every five men and five out of every hundred women are ruptured as a result of their own or somebody else's recklessness.

On the top of nearly every house in the section where *artesian* water is used, there is a *tank* to receive water for various purposes about each dwelling; much of this is employed for drinking and culinary uses. Without any attempt at a sensation, we pronounce this box or *tank* a *death trap!* There is not a clean one in this whole great city, that has an outside exposure, and 9 out of every 10 are reeking with filth. Having had occasion to investigate several I am convinced that they average alike. If so, there are at least 500 tons of concentrated filth playing the part of filters in the tanks of this city alone at this writing! And there is every reason to believe that this city is as clean as the average. Provided this is so, there is enough of such refuse in the United States to dam the Mississippi River many times and build a levee across Lake Erie.

Health officers may keep their own tanks clean in the future, but if individuals desire health and abolition of the need of Health Boards, let them keep their own tanks, back yards, streets, and pavements neat. Municipal corporations should prevent by *law* the throwing of any kind of rubbish into the streets, and make it a misdemeanor for the proprietors allowing any of their mercantile houses, work-shops, or residences to be found filthy, and there are thousands of them in this city. To avoid accidents, every man, woman, and child should be compelled to pass to their right on the street. Every person in every city not having a legitimate vocation in the eyes of the law, nor an income from property or money in the bank, should, if criminally inclined, be sent to the House of Correction. If poor and willing to work, they ought to be put to work in the public streets and in the parks, to beautify them, for the benefit of the frugal classes. No begging should be allowed, under penalty of imprisonment. That a city may escape being overrun by country tramps, their entrance should be quarantined.

To stop contagion, public *crematories* should be established and cremation of the human and animal bodies be compulsory. If the principal church and secret organizations will now change their rituals so as to permit of the incineration of the bodies of their deceased members, the world will have advanced 100 years before the close of this century and the average duration of life at that date will have increased from 34.8 to 40 years. It is needful that the false sentiment regarding the disposition of our dead should undergo a complete revolution. There could probably be no better aid to this end than a general investigation of the mortuary records of the towns and cities of the globe, by proper officials, the facts and discoveries of whom should be given all possible publicity. An hundred or so years ago this was not so much a matter of importance as now, with a greater and increasing density of population, by virtue of which a great portion of the habitable earth is fast becoming a mass of putrifying corruption, that will involve at no distant time the world in pestilence, woe, and desolation.

The recent official return on the condition of the London cemeteries is, or should be, sufficient to cause all reasonable persons to cry out for the crematory. In Brompton Cemetery, with an area of twenty-eight and three-fourths of an acre, there have been buried in less than fifty years one hundred and fifty-five thousand bodies. In Tower Hamlets Cemetery, with twelve acres less, in about the same time, the number is two hundred and forty-seven thousand.

When it is remembered how perfectly unfitted the soil of these districts is for burial purposes, together with the means so largely employed for preventing speedy decomposition, one may readily imagine the danger that menaces those above this still-increasing mass of sub-pollution.

Multiply the condition of the London suburbs by several hundred thousand more, and then ponder the product! Talk about sanitary regulations, when our public health laws are violated thus, and the air and water poisoned as a result of the superstitious custom of body burial! When pestilence stalks abroad, it is said to be planetary influence or divine wrath! The following from the Springfield *Republican* will indicate the current of public opinion: —

"That the custom of burying the dead is bound to be superseded by more scientific and economical methods, especially in the centers of population, may be seen in the reanimation of the old scheme of desiccation by New York capitalists. These men are not yet ready to accept cremation. Their project is to build mausoleums as substitutes for cemeteries, where the body will be subjected to the absorbent action of currents of pure, dry air, which will prevent decomposition, and, by thoroughly exhausting the body of moisture and gases, carry away all germs of disease. These air currents, thus laden, will then pass through furnaces, where all noxious elements will be destroyed. The lifeless form will be reduced in weight about two-thirds and nearly one-half in size. Resting in a sepulcher, it may then be preserved for an indefinite period. As explained in detail, with particulars of the beauty of the buildings thrown in, this scheme has advantages compared with the undesirable method in vogue, though it is less thorough and simple than cremation. A promoter of the enterprise in speaking of the desiccated body says that 'although shrunken, still, with the semblance of life, it is an object that the eye of affection can look upon without a shock, and the sanitarian can think of without a shudder.' In essence, however, the scheme is simply a concession to a public, not yet educated to the idea of cremation. While appropriating enough of the latter system to solve the question of public health, it caters to the human sentimentalities in preserving at half size the dead form. Upon these sentiments, summed up as the 'instinct of humanity,' the promoters of the new system base their hopes of profit. Besides advancing in its favor all the arguments used for cremation, its friends add that in the desiccating process no danger can exist of suspended animation escaping notice."

Public *fountains* should be established in every other block of cities or towns having over 1,000 inhabitants, with best-devised filters known, so that both man and beast could enjoy pure water to drink, free for the taking. During epidemics it should be not only compulsory in municipalities to have water filtered in each house before drinking, but it should be boiled. Every house ought to have a filter. If you cannot afford a $40 one, you can secure one for 40 cents.

CHAPTER VII.

"Vice is a monster of so frightful mien,
As to be hated, needs but to be seen;
Yet seen too oft, familiar with her face,
We first endure, then pity, then embrace."

"But evil is wrought by want of thought
As well as by want of heart."

The following extract from the report of the Grand Jury of this city, given publicity December 5, 1889, is self-explanatory:—

"Some of the dives and variety theaters are the nurseries of vice and crime, where drunkenness is encouraged, our youth demoralized, the unwary roped in and robbed, and crimes committed which the authorities are unable to prevent or discover. There is, of course, a broad distinction to be noted between those places of public resort where the demand for distilled, fermented, and malt liquors is supplied in a legitimate manner, and the entertainment provided, if any, is not of an objectionable character, and those places where salacious performances are presented as an attraction, and lewd women, under the guise of waitresses to serve liquors, pursue a shameful vocation. These evils may be partly remedied if respectable citizens will refuse to rent their property for such uses, and also refuse to assist in obtaining licenses whereby such headquarters for drunkenness, lewdness, and crime are in a measure entrenched behind existing general laws.

"The so-called 'social evil' is aggressive on our thoroughfares, and should be restrained by the authorities within narrower limits."

But we add our interpretation and our suggestions for these twin evils which stalk up and down the earth and apparently defy control.

The *minister* treats lightly upon the liquor traffic, in many instances because certain of his church members either sell it at wholesale, retail, or furnish the barley, corn, grapes, hops, or rent to the man who does. The *editors* of all newspapers of general circulation must treat the subject likewise, for fear of his advertising patrons. His readers are never taken into account, for the simple reason that circulation alone does not pay newspapers issued daily, and very few that are issued weekly. It will be seen by the above report that the grand jurymen too have *vital* interests at stake. In order to keep their respective businesses from being boycotted by their fellow-merchants, they handle the subject with soft gloves, as if it were eggs, and the "social evil" by this same jury is done up in *nineteen* words. But they have indicated a great deal in those few words, namely, that such an evil *does exist*—something the different *church* organizations have *refused* to acknowledge.

High license, with personal responsibility for results, under a sufficient bond, will in time remedy the liquor traffic.

The *social evil* should be licensed, and under the perfect control of the police—and not the police under its control, as seems to be the case in this city. Are they not under pay to look the other way? Its boundaries should be exact, isolated, and under the direct supervision of the health department. Is there any justice in demanding a license of a milliner, or on any other mercantile pursuit that a female may see fit to adopt, while 5,000 of these questionable women go untaxed, because you do not *dare* to acknowledge that their calling *exists?* To ask the question is to answer it—No!! Let no one think that in any way whatever we would seem to unduly countenance, or in the least encourage, this evil. But we do believe in recognizing absolute facts. They cannot be overlooked. It is surprising that, amidst all this widespread discussion of intemperance, no more has been said on this *social problem*. As long as men are mortal, this condition of relations will exist—it has existed through all time—but it is possible to limit it, to heavily license it, and keep it within proper bounds.

Then by all means should churches and various kinds of societies exert their influence to the legal recognition of the true status, and benefit the general condition of mankind. Boards of supervisors, aldermen, etc., are clothed with power to accomplish the ends suggested, if they are only backed by public sentiment.

If the *Catholic Church* organization alone will inaugurate a general agitation over the country, as they have already indicated and begun in their convention at Baltimore, on the liquor traffic, they will either break it up or put it under control; for 60% of this business is carried on by their following.

Public *urinals* are greater necessities than public fountains in cities and large towns. The alarming increase of *diabetes* and kidney troubles in cities during the last few years, while remaining normal, or actually decreasing in the rural districts, has led to the belief that the prolonged detention of the urine is the principal, and, in most cases, the only cause of this terrible malady. The foregoing facts recapitulated exhibit a few of the ills of mankind that are in the power of municipal officials to alleviate. The duties of the general government cover all of the above, and include the *prevention* of all *criminals* and *paupers* of every nation from *landing* on our shores; the compulsory education of all citizens old and young—as it is cheaper to educate than to punish criminals; to furnish employment upon all useful and needed public works for the worthy, willing poor, and cause to be distributed with equity to the deserving, all the earnings of the criminal institutions of the country, over and above their actual expenses.

It will not be out of place to complete this chapter with a few words on the necessity of giving man and beast *one day* in seven to *rest. Sunday* seems to be the preferable one, but to compel the observance of one particular day in each week for all classes and sects would be tyrannical. The majority of religious societies employ Sunday for worship and rest, but, throwing aside the moral and religious bearing, every human being would be healthier, happier, and live longer, if he rested one day in the week. We all live too fast. Though we enjoy laziness at times, yet we are too anxious to get riches or fame earlier than we ought or can. A man may work so mightily that he will be very wealthy at 40 instead of 50, but he will die at 70 instead of 80. Better prolong life by reserving forces for the future.

CHAPTER VIII.

"For a man's house is his castle."

After individual cleanliness and regularity, erect your next *house* in which you intend to live, or that you expect to rent to another, or remodel your present residence, to correspond with the following:—

SANITARY HOUSE.—It should stand facing the sun, on dry soil, in a wide, clean, amply-sewered, substantially-paved street, over a deep, thoroughly ventilated and lighted cellar. The floor of the cellar should be cemented, the walls and ceilings plastered and thickly whitewashed with lime every year, that the house may not act as a chimney to draw up into its chambers micro-organisms from the earth. If your lot is situated so that you cannot face your house either east or south, construct the rooms in such a way that your parlors and sleeping apartments will receive the sun at least 3 hours during the day. All windows should extend from floor to ceiling, adjusted to let down from the top, and in position to secure as much as possible of the through currents of air. The outside walls, if of wood or brick, should be kept thickly painted, not to shut out penetrating air, but for the sake of dryness. All inside walls should be plastered smooth, painted, and, however unaesthetic, varnished. Mantels should be of marble, plate, iron, or, if wood, plain, and, whether natural, painted, or stained, varnished.

Interior wood-work, including floors, should all show plain surfaces and be likewise treated. No paper on the walls, no carpets on the floors, but movable rugs, which can be shaken daily in the open air—not at doors or out of windows, where dust is blown back into rooms—should cover the floors. White linen shades, which will soon show the necessity of washing, should protect the windows. All furniture should be plain, with cane seats, without upholstery. Mattresses should be covered with oiled silk. Blankets, sheets, and spreads—no comforts or quilts—should constitute the bedding.

Of plumbing there should be as little as is necessary, and all there is must be exposed.

The inhabited rooms should be heated only with open fires, the cellar and halls by radiated heat, or, better, by a hot-air furnace, which shall take its fresh air from above the top of the house and not from the cellar itself or the surface of the earth, where micro-organisms most abound. Let there be no annual house cleaning, but keep it clean all the time, and have it gone through thoroughly at least four times per year.

Of course a corner lot is always preferable, but how often it is supposed that the benefit consists alone in a commanding position, in a chance for architectural display, when the greatest boon is the increased opportunity for sunlight. The atmosphere of a room where the sun never shines is never agreeable or healthful. Science has taught us that the sun is the source of all life. It will effect more than tons of disinfectants and chemicals to purge and sweeten the air of a house. Let the building be exposed to the south, and keep shade trees from checking the sun too much. Verandas and broad piazzas often do as much harm as they give pleasure—especially if they are all covered with vines. Be more careful about plumbing than people are wont to be. Do not practice economy by trying to cut down *plumbing* bills. When a contractor agrees to erect a house, either withhold this part from him or see that he employs the most skilled labor. Ventilation cannot be slighted, for upon it health greatly depends. If you can in any way afford it, use *incandescent electric light* instead of gas or oil. The reason is a powerful one. An ordinary *gas* jet destroys as much pure air and oxygen as five men—a good-sized *oil lamp* equal to three men. Add to this the heat that comes from such methods, and we see the strong advantage of the incandescent electric light. This vitiates no air, gives off no perceptible heat. Though there are stories that electric lights injure the eyes, from careful observation we find that it hurts the eyes of the majority no more than any artificial light.

The *Sanitary News* urges people not to paper or paint the interior walls of houses. Arsenical poisons are used in coloring wall paper. Mold collects in flour paste used in fastening paper to walls, absorbing moisture and germs of disease. Glue also disintegrates, so that any friction removes small particles, to which germs attach and float in the air. Undecorated walls, ugly as they are, the *News* insists are the only healthy ones to live within.

Dr. Cushing, of this city, thus ends his lecture on "Healthful Houses":—

"The essentials then of good house building are, first, a dry soil, a good foundation, exposure to the sun, and, next, good plumbing by reputable men at whatever cost necessary for first-class work, warming and ventilating by open grates rather than by steam heaters and stoves, clean floors and clean walls; and now, if there be no decomposition of animal or vegetable matter allowed in the immediate vicinity of the house, we shall have done the best that the present state of science will permit toward making our houses healthful."

The Hotel Del Monte is the only perfectly clean hotel in America. It is located at Monterey, Cal., not over a quarter of a mile from the ocean. The prevailing winds are from the sea and would naturally blow over the sands towards the house. Now the cause of dirt has virtually been killed by the planting of trees, brush, and by the laying of asphaltum walks and sod-ground drives on this windward side. The only dirt is that which is brought there by travelers—this is easily kept down. The moral is here: If possible prevent dust and dirt by stopping the cause.

CHAPTER IX.

"Let this great maxim be my virtue's guide."

As we are hastily reading books and papers we continually come across maxims, epigrams, and short, pithy sayings that attract us. We wish we could not only remember them, but also often put them in practice, but they slip our mind and actions almost immediately. From time to time the author has collected fruit from the vast field of health of its kindred subjects, and placed the best of them in this book for the reader's careful consideration. Among the multitude of "Don'ts" for politeness are the following for health alone:—

"Don't endeavor to rest the mind by absolute inactivity; let it seek its rest in work in other channels, and thus rest the tired part of the brain.

"Don't delude yourself into the belief that you are an exception as far as sleep is concerned; the normal average of sleep is eight hours.

"Don't allow your servants to put meat and vegetables in the same compartments of the refrigerator.

"Don't keep the parlor dark unless you value your carpet more than your and your children's health.

"Don't forget that moral defects are as often the cause as they are the effects of physical faults.

"Don't direct special mental or physical energies to more than eight hours' work in each day.

"Don't neglect to have your dentist examine your teeth at least every three months.

"Don't read, write, or do any delicate work unless receiving the light from the left side.

"Don't pamper the appetite with such variety of food that may lead to excess.

"Don't read in street-cars or other jolting vehicles.

"Don't eat or drink hot and cold things immediately in succession.

"Don't pick the teeth with pins or any other hard substance.

"Don't sleep in a room provided with stationary washstands.

"Don't neglect any opportunity to insure a variety of food."

There are many things we should *never* do. Among them are:—

"Never go to bed with cold or damp feet.

"Never lean with the back upon anything that is cold.

"Never begin a journey until the breakfast has been eaten.

"Never take warm drinks and then immediately go out in the cold.

"Never ride in an open carriage or near the window of a car for a moment after exercise; it is dangerous to health or even life.

"Never omit regular bathing, for unless the skin is in regular condition the cold will close the pores and favor congestion or other diseases.

"Never stand still in cold weather, especially after having taken a slight degree of exercise."

Perhaps among the following you may find succinctly stated what will be of eminent value:—

"Focus your brain as you would a burning-glass. Butter enough for a slice won't do for a whole loaf.

"Keep empty-headed between times. Mental furniture should be very select. Useless lumber in the upper story is worse than a pocketful of oyster shells. Leave your facts on your book shelves, where you can find them when wanted. A walking encyclopedia cannot work for want of room to turn round in his own head.

"Don't tax your memory. Make a memorandum, and put it in your pocket. Every unnecessary thought is a waste of effective force.

"Don't believe that muscular exercise contracts head work. Brain and muscle are bung-hole and spigot of the same barrel. It is poor economy to keep both running.

"Pin your faith to the genius of hard work. It is the safest, most reliable, and most manageable sort of genius.

"Amuse yourself. This is the first principle of good hard work. And the second is like unto it.

"Don't work too much. It is quantity, not quality, that kills. Therefore, work only in the day-time. Night was made for sleep. And loaf on Sunday. Six days' work earns the right to go a-fishing, or to church, or to any harmless diversion, on the seventh.

"Go to work promptly, but slowly. A late, hurried start keeps you out of breath all day trying to catch up.

"When you stop work forget it. It spoils brains to simmer after a hard boil.

"Feed regularly, largely, and slowly. Lose no meal; approach it respectfully and give it gratefully. No more can be got out of a man than is put into him.

"Sleep one-third of your whole life. How I hate the moralist who croaks over time wasted in sleep. Besides, sleep is, on the whole, the most satisfactory mode of existence."

MISCONCEIVEMENTS.—"There are a number of mistakes made even by wise people while passing through life. Prominent among them is the idea that you must labor when you are not in a fit condition to do so; to think that the more a person eats the healthier and stronger he will become; to go to bed at midnight and rise at daybreak, and imagine that every hour taken from sleep is an hour gained; to imagine that, if a little work or exercise is good, violent and prolonged exercise is better; to conclude that the smallest room in the house is large enough to sleep in; to eat as if you had only a moment to finish a meal in, or to eat without any appetite, or to continue after it has been satisfied, merely to please the taste; to believe that children can do as much work as grown people, and that the more hours they study the more they learn; to imagine that whatever remedy causes one to feel immediately better (as alcoholic stimulants) is good for the system, without regard to the after-effects; to take off proper clothing out of season because you have become heated; to sleep exposed to a direct draught; to think any nostrum or patent medicine is a specific for all the diseases flesh is heir to."

WEARINESS.—"A tramp knows what it is to be leg-weary, a farm laborer to be body-weary, a literary man to be brain-weary, and a sorrowing man to be soul-weary. The sick are often weary of life itself. Weariness is generally a physiological 'ebb-tide,' which time and patience will convert into a 'flow'. It is never well to whip or spur a worn-out horse, except in the direst straits. If he mends his pace in obedience to the stimulus, every step is a drop drawn from his life-blood. Idleness is not one of the faults of the present age; weariness is one of the commonest experiences. The checks that many a man draws on his physiological resources are innumerable; and, as these resources are strictly limited, like any other ordinary banking account, it is very easy to bring about a balance on the wrong side. Adequate rest is one kind of repayment to the bank, sound sleep is another, regular eating and good digestion another. One day's holiday in the week and one or two months in the year for those who work exceptionally hard usually bring the credit balance to a highly favorable condition; and thus with care and management physiological solvency is secured and maintained."

"WHAT PRODUCES DEATH.—Someone says that few men die of age. Almost all persons die of disappointment, personal, mental, or bodily toil, or accident. The passions kill men sometimes even suddenly. The common expression, 'choked with passion,' has little exaggeration in it, for even though not suddenly fatal, strong passions shorten life. Strong-bodied men often die young; weak men live longer than the strong, for the strong use their strength and the weak have none to use. The latter take care of themselves, the former do not. As it is with the body, so it is with the mind and temper. The strong are apt to break, or, like the candle, run; the weak burn out. The inferior animals, which live temperate lives, have generally their prescribed term of years. The horse lives 25 years, the ox 15 or 20, the lion about 20, the hog 10 or 12, the rabbit 8, the guinea-pig 6 or 7. The numbers all bear proportion to the time the animal takes to grow to its full size. But man, of all animals, is one that seldom comes up to the average.

He ought to live a hundred years, according to the physiological law, for five times 20 are 100; but instead of that he scarcely reaches an average of four times the growing period. The reason is obvious—man is not only the most irregular and most intemperate, but the most laborious and hard-working of all animals. He is always the most irritable of all animals, and there is reason to believe, though we cannot tell what an animal secretly feels, that more than any other animal man cherishes wrath to keep it warm, and consumes himself with the fire of his own reflections."

Provided you have babies in your family go through the following and see if you can't train your child so it shall be among the last seventeen mentioned:—

"Take your pencil and follow me, while we figure on what will happen to the 1,000,000 of babies that will have been born in the last 1,000,000 seconds.

"I believe that is about the average—'one every time the clock ticks.'

"One year hence, if statistics don't belie us, we will have lost 150,000 of these little 'prides of the household.'

"A year later 53,000 more will be keeping company with those that have gone before.

"At the end of the third year we find that 22,000 more have dropped by the wayside.

"The fourth year they have become rugged little darlings, not nearly so susceptible to infantile diseases, only 8,000 having succumbed to the rigors imposed by the master.

"By the time they have arrived at the age of twelve years but a paltry few hundred leave the track each year.

"After threescore years have come and gone we find less trouble in counting the army with which we started in the fall of 1889.

"Of the 1,000,000 with which we began our count, but 370,000 remain; 630,000 have gone the way of all the world, and the remaining few have forgotten that they ever existed. At the end of eighty, or, taking our mode of reckoning, by the year 1969 A. D., there are still 97,000 gray-haired, shaky old grannies and grandfathers, toothless, hairless, and happy.

"In the year 1984 our 1,000,000 babies with which we started in 1889 will have dwindled to an insignificant 223 helpless old wrecks, 'stranded on the shores of time.'

"In 1992 all but seventeen have left this mundane sphere forever, while the last remaining wreck will probably, in seeming thoughtlessness, watch the sands filter through the hour-glass of time, and die in the year 1997 at the age of one hundred and eight.

"What a bounteous supply of food for reflection!"

"LAUGHTER AS A HEALTH PROMOTER.—In his 'Problem of Health,' Dr. Greene says that there is not the remotest corner or little inlet of the minute blood-vessels of the human body that does not feel some wavelet from the convulsions occasioned by good hearty laughter. The life principle, or the central man, is shaken to its innermost depths, sending new tides of life and strength to the surface, thus materially tending to insure good health to the persons who indulge therein. The blood moves more rapidly and conveys a different impression to all the organs of the body, as it visits them on that particular mystic journey when the man is laughing, from what it does at other times. For this reason every good hearty laugh in which a person indulges tends to lengthen his life, conveying, as it does, new and distinct stimulus to the vital forces."

CHAPTER X.

"While bright-eyed science watches round."

A scientific investigation into the nature and causes of consumption proves the immediate causes, apart from hereditary, to be dampness of houses and localities. Of races, the negroes seem most liable, and the Jews the most exempt. A french scientist has found that inhalation of air containing a small amount of *hydrofluoric acid* gas has a remarkably good effect on *consumption*. In England good results were obtained by inspiration of air mixed with *ozone*. That the disease results chiefly from inactivity of the lungs is the statement of a physician who maintains that the cure of the disease is a mechanical question. The International Tuberculosis Congress lately held at Paris admits that tuberculosis is contagious, can be transmitted from man to animals, and *vice versa*, and is the same in men, women, and cattle. Diseased milk is the most frequent agent of transmission, and with this meat, particularly lightly cooked, as food. Predisposing causes are sedentary life, overwork, mental anxiety, insufficient nourishment, in general, anything calculated to lower the vitality. The congress has discovered no remedy, only palliatives for tuberculosis. Catarrhs, bronchitis, and other throat troubles have a tendency to develop into pleurisy or consumption when neglected.

Typhoid fever never affects the atmosphere, but it does affect water, milk, ice, and meat. The eggs of a parasite from dogs, and hence more or less infecting all waters to which dogs have access, appear to have an unequaled facility of passage to all parts of the human system.

As for *surgical operations,* in a German paper are particulars of a case in which the eye of a man was thrust out of its socket by a parasite cyst in the rear, discovered by surgical exploration and extracted. From a 5-year old boy an injured kidney was removed successfully and the patient recovered. The bridge of the nose was completely restored by using the breast-bone of a chicken and stretching the flesh of the old nose over it.

Even the part of a destroyed nerve of the arm was restored by the substitution of a part of a sound nerve from an amputated limb, so that the continuity was restored and sensation returned in 36 hours! Prematurely-born children are kept in an artificial mother, which consists of a glass case warmed by bowls of water. A new opiate has been discovered called the sulsonal. It produces sleep in nervous people and those affected with heart disease, but not in healthy subjects. The idea that sufferers from heart disease should avoid physical exertion has been dispelled by a noted physiologist who has successfully employed regulated exercise.

Brown-Séquard has brought out his great Vital Fluid. He is reported as saying: "I never made use of the word 'elixir,' still less of the words 'elixir of life.' These are all expressions or inventions of sensational newspapers. If quacks or ignorant men in America have killed people, as stated by the New York papers, they would have avoided committing those murders had they paid the least attention to the most elementary rules as regards the subcutaneous injection of animal substances. Injections of animal matter have no danger, as a rule, unless the substances begin to be decomposed. When this condition of things exists, no good can be obtained, and there is grave danger of inflammation, abscesses, and even death."

"Professor Brown-Séquard is reported to have lately informed the French Academy of Sciences that, by condensing the watery vapor coming from the human lungs, he obtained a poisonous liquid capable of producing almost immediate death. The poison is an alkaloid (organic), and not a microbe or series of microbes. He injected this liquid under the skin of a rabbit and the effect was speedily mortal without convulsions. Dr. Séquard said it was fully proved that respired air contains a volatile element far more dangerous than the carbonic acid which is one of its constituents, and that the human breath contains a highly poisonous agent. This startling fact should be borne in mind by the occupants of crowded horse-cars and ill-ventilated apartments."

"A very curious geographical distribution of certain virtues and vices has been mooted by a scientist. Intemperance is mostly found above latitude 48°, amatory aberrations south of the forty-fifth, financial extravagance in large seaports, industrial thrift, in pastoral highland regions."

"Advance in Hygienic Clothing.—The new cellular clothing now coming into use in England is said to be a success. It is woven out of the same materials as the common weaves of cloth, being simply, as its name indicates, closely woven into cells, the network of which is covered over with a thin fluff. Its porous quality allows the slow passing of the outside and inside air, giving time for the outside air to become of the same temperature as the body, obviating all danger of catching colds, and allowing vapors constantly exhaled by the body to pass off, thus contributing toward health and cleanliness. The common objection to cotton clothing—that it is productive of chills and colds—is removed if woven in this manner, and the invention can certainly be said to be strictly in accordance with hygienic and scientific principles."

The annual death rate, in 1888, for the principal cities of the world, per 1,000 inhabitants, was: San Francisco, Cleveland, Stockholm, 17; Bristol, Dresden, 18; Chicago, Cincinnati, Edinburgh, London, Turin, 19; Berlin, Baltimore, Brussels, Buffalo, Liverpool, Philadelphia, Pittsburg, 20; Brooklyn, St. Louis, Tokyo, 21; Amsterdam, Christiana, Paris, Washington, 22; Glasgow, 23; Copenhagen, 24; Bombay, Boston, New Orleans, Pesth, Venice, Vienna, 25; Breslau, Calcutta, Manchester, New York, Prague, Rotterdam, 26; Dublin, 27; Rome, 28; Hamburg, Munich, 29; Trieste, 30; Buda Pesth, St. Petersburg, 32; Alexandria, 38; Madras, 40; and Cairo, 51.

The death rate among the poor and rich respectively varies much. In Paris the death rate per 1,000 inhabitants between 40 and 50 years in easy circumstances was 8.3 against 18.7 among the poor. In London are some districts of the wealthy classes where the rate was 11.3 against 38 in the slums. The mean age at death among the gentry was 55 years, while among the workers it was 20-1/2 years. It was found that only 8% of the children of the upper classes died in their first year against 19% in the general population of Liverpool and 33% in the slums of that city. Deaths from consumption were nearly one-fourth of all deaths among the poor, and only one-eighteenth among the rich.

The above facts and figures cannot fail to set every intelligent person who reads them to thinking of this great health problem.

CHAPTER XI.

HAPPINESS.

"The learned is happy Nature to explore,
The fool is happy that he knows no more."

Happiness is defined by Webster as an agreeable feeling or condition of the soul arising from good of any kind; the possession of those circumstances or that state of being which is attended with enjoyment; the state of being happy; felicity; blessedness: bliss; joyful satisfaction.

Happiness is generic and applied to almost every kind of enjoyment except that of the animal appetites; *felicity* is a more formal word, and is used more sparingly in the same general sense, but with elevated associations; *blessedness* is applied to the most refined enjoyment arising from the purest social, benevolent, and religious affections; *bliss* denotes still more exalted delight, and is applied more appropriately to the joy anticipated in heaven.

Happiness is only comparative, and we drink it in, in the exact ratio of our understanding to interpret the justice of the divinity within us. The first prerequisite is *wisdom*, the second is like unto it, *more wisdom*, and the third sufficient understanding to know that it is wisdom.

"It is easy enough to be pleasant,
   When life flows by like a song,
But the man worth while is one who will smile
   When everything goes dead wrong.
For the test of the heart is trouble,
   And it always comes with the years,
And the smile that is worth the praises of earth
   Is the smile that shines through tears.

"It is easy enough to be prudent
   When nothing tempts you to stray,
When without or within no voice of sin

Is luring your soul away.
But it's only a negative virtue
   Until it is tried by fire,
And the life that is worth the honor of earth
   Is the one that resists desire.

"By the cynic, the sad, the fallen,
   Who had no strength for the strife,
The world's highway is cumbered to-day,
   They make up the item of life,
But the virtue that conquers passion,
   And the sorrow that hides in a smile,
It is these that are worth the homage of earth,
   For we find them but once in a while."

—*Ella Wheeler Wilcox.*

We possess none of the attributes save in a degree only, any one of which can be intensified, brightened, or benefited by our thoughts and actions. The shortest road to happiness, after having cleansed your body, actions, and thoughts, is to "do all the good you can, in all the ways you can, to all living creatures you can, just as long as you can." The more unselfish you become, the less you think of personal comfort, and the more pleasure you take in the comforts of others, the deeper and broader will the fountains of your own happiness become. There is no class of people who have equal happiness or bliss pictured upon their countenances to those who practice and teach the universal brotherhood of man without regard to race, creed, sex, caste, or color.

Happiness is like manna. It is to be "gathered in grains and enjoyed every day; it will not keep; it cannot be accumulated; nor need we go out of ourselves nor into remote places to gather it, since it is rained down from heaven at our very doors, or, rather, within them."

George Macdonald says: "A man must not choose his neighbor; he must take the neighbor that God sends him. In him, whoever he be, lies hidden or revealed a beautiful brother. Any rough-hewn semblance of humanity will at length be enough to move the man to reverence and affection."

And there is a still more extensive love, urges Charles Mackay:—

"You love your fellow-creatures? So do I,—
But underneath the wide paternal sky
Are there no fellow-creatures in your ken
That you can love except your fellow-men?
Are not the grass, the flowers, the trees, the birds,
The faithful beasts, true-hearted, without words,
Your fellows also, howsoever small?
He's the best lover who can love them all."

There are certain principles that lead to positive happiness. One of these is the avoiding of mistakes. "What have been termed 'the fourteen mistakes of life' are given as follows: It is a great mistake to set up our own standard of right and wrong and judge people accordingly; to measure the enjoyment of others by our own; to expect uniformity of opinion in this world; to look for judgment and experience in youth; to endeavor to mould all dispositions alike; not to yield to immaterial trifles; to look for perfection in our own actions; to worry ourselves and others with what cannot be remedied; not to alleviate all that needs alleviation as far as lies in our power; not to make allowances for the infirmities of others; to consider everything impossible that we cannot perform; to believe only what our finite minds can grasp; to expect to be able to understand everything. The greatest of mistakes is to live for time alone when any moment may launch us into eternity."

Ignorance is a state of happiness that many fairly intellectual people cite as well worthy of emulation; but those who assert it have not understood, or attempted to fathom, how shallow is this lake of knownothingness called "ignorance." Only a slight ripple can be seen on the bosom of a shallow lake during the most fearful storm, yet but a slight zephyr is needed to show the white caps upon the grand old ocean, and at the least provocation of a storm "see how she causes the continents to tremble, showing her great depth and majesty." If in the presence of this happy, ignorant personage, we place the most beautiful piece of statuary or painting, or produce the most startling of Shakespeare's plays, with the best living talent, or have the most gifted vocalist sing the most difficult *aria*, or have a panorama of the pyramid Jeezeh, Eiffel Tower, Washington Monument, Philadelphia City Hall, Cologne Cathedral, all actual size, and such of nature's grandest views as the Yosemite Fall, and Father of the Forest, we would look upon this happy individual and listen in breathless silence for his opinion. Well, what of it? what is to prevent it? would be the reply. But note the difference even in a cultured child; see the gentle cheek turn from pale pink to livid carmine, the heart pant, the bosom heave, and the whole form, for the time being, feel itself suspended in the air. To the above picture, add cultured, ripe old age, and the enjoyment, ecstasy, and pure happiness that would follow could only be measured by the difference between where *we* stand and the *end* of space!

Prerequisites in the begetting of wisdom are, first, you must be regular in everything you do, act, or think. This will give you health. Second, you must be regular, cleanly, temperate, and moral. This will start you on the road to happiness. Third, in addition to the first and second propositions, you must exercise self-control in all its aspects if you would have health, be happy, and live to excessive old age, before the culmination of which you will possess wisdom of no ordinary character.

Let the legend that "man's inhumanity to man makes countless thousands mourn," cease, and in its place have, "The universal brotherhood of man removes the shackles of inhumanity, replacing them by bands of love." This will elevate the trend of human thought, and every zephyr of human intellect will gather and multiply until a cyclone of happiness envelopes the earth; like love it will seem but a soothing breeze to the human heart, so gentle will fall its benign influences.

This brings us to the point where every person is led to look to each of the four points of the compass and there exclaim, "Who or what is God?" This is the first thing upon which intelligent beings should render a decision; mankind can only approximate happiness until they have settled in their own mind this point. It is not imperative that your decision should cover *all* the truth or the *only* truth in regard to Deity, but it should preclude all doubt on the part of the person so deciding. There is just as much inconsistency in the statement that we know who and what is God in his physical proportions, just where He or It resides, and just what relation It or He holds toward the human monad, man, as there is in the assertion, "There is no God."

There is no harm, however, in asserting our belief in *one* God, the Trinity, or a great First Cause. If we believe it and shape our lives accordingly, true light will be given sufficient to satisfy each searcher after the Truth; and he or they will advance to some other belief just when it is necessary. The exultant Methodist receives his light in one form, and the quiet Quaker in another. The devout Catholic represents still another type of ritualistic form, and the Wisdom Religionist (Theosophist) seems to get his from Nature, and finds some good in everything. With the 1,100 other different kinds of faith, there should be no complaint on our part of a variety from which to choose.

We offer not as anything new, but as something possibly forgotten, the following formulæ for obtaining happiness, *viz.*: (1) The carrying out in our lives and actions the Golden Rule; (2) total unselfishness as regards self; (3) trying to excel all others in doing what the world calls *good*; (4) condemning no one until we have heard both sides of the question in dispute; (5) having the same tender compassion for all the lower animals that you exercise towards the human family; (6) following out consistently some religious belief, and, until you are convinced of a better one, defending it; (7) above all other things, having charity for every person's short-comings and belief. Add to these a few intrinsic principles: (1) Happiness is no other than soundness and perfection of mind; (2) there are two ways of being happy—we may either diminish our wants or augment our means—either will do, the result is the same; and it is for each man to decide for himself, and do that which happens to be the easiest; (3) happiness is a road-side flower growing on the highways of usefulness; (4) carry the radiance of your soul in your face; let the world have the benefit of it; (5) learn the lesson embodied in this little poem:—

THE TWO WORKERS.

"Two workers in one field
   Toiled on from day to day,
Both had the same hard labor,
   Both had the same small pay;
With the same blue sky above,
   The same green grass below,
One soul was full of love,

   The other full of woe.

"One leaped up with the light,
   With the soaring of the lark;
One felt it ever night,
   For his soul was ever dark.
One heart was hard as stone,
   One heart was ever gay;
One worked with many a groan,
   One whistled all the day.

"One had a flower-clad cot
   Beside a merry mill;
Wife and children near the spot
   Made it sweeter, fairer still.
One a wretched hovel had,
   Full of discord, dirt, and din,
No wonder he seemed mad,
   Wife and children starved within.

"Still they worked in the same field,
   Toiled on from day to day,
Both had the same hard labor,
   Both had the same small pay;
But they worked not with one will:
   The reason let me tell—
Lo! the one drank at the still,
   And the other at the well."

(6) Embody in your lives the better idea of this poem, "Where Do You Live," by Josephine Pollard:—

"I knew a man, and his name was Horner,
Who used to live on Grumble Corner:
Grumble Corner, in Cross-Patch Town,
And he was never seen without a frown.
He grumbled at this; he grumbled at that;
He growled at the dog; he growled at the cat;

He grumbled at morning; he grumbled at night;
And to grumble and growl were his chief delight.

"He grumbled so much at his wife that she
Began to grumble as well as he;
And all the children, wherever they went,
Reflected their parents' discontent.
If the sky was dark and betokened rain,
Then Mr. Horner was sure to complain;
And, if there was never a cloud about,
He'd grumble because of a threatened drought.

"His meals were never to suit his taste;
He grumbled at having to eat in haste;
The bread was poor, or the meat was tough,
Or else he hadn't had half enough.
No matter how hard his wife might try
To please her husband, with scornful eye
He'd look around, and then, with a scowl
At something or other, begin to growl.

"One day, as I loitered about the street,
My old acquaintance I chanced to meet,
Whose face was without the look of care
And the ugly frown which it used to wear.
'I may be mistaken, perhaps,' I said,
As, after saluting, I turned my head;
'But it is, and it isn't, the Mr. Horner
Who lived for so long on Grumble Corner!'

"I met him next day; and I met him again,
In melting weather, and pouring rain,
When stocks were up and when stocks were down;
But a smile somehow had replaced the frown.
It puzzled me much; and so one day
I seized his hand in a friendly way,
And said: 'Mr. Horner, I'd like to know

What can have happened to change you so?'

"He laughed a laugh that was good to hear,
For it told of a conscience calm and clear,
And he said, with none of the old-time drawl,
'Why, I've changed my residence, that is all!'
'Changed your residence?' 'Yes,' said Horner,
'It wasn't healthy on Grumble Corner,
And so I moved; 'twas a change complete;
And you'll find me now on Thanksgiving Street!'

"Now, every day as I move along
The streets so filled with the busy throng,
I watch each face and can always tell
Where men and women and children dwell;
And many a discontented mourner
Is spending his days on Grumble Corner,
Sour and sad, whom I long to entreat
To take a house on Thanksgiving Street."

CHAPTER XII.

"Gold can gild a rotten stick and dirt sully an ingot."

AIDS TO MORALITY.—"Many imagine that the only ways in which public and private morality can be improved," says the Philadelphia *Ledger*, "are those definite and direct methods which appeal at once to the conscience and the heart. Preaching and teaching, persuading and warning, exhorting and encouraging, are instrumentalities worthy of all honor, and those whose abilities qualify them for such tasks should receive every possible stimulus to exert them in so noble a cause. But it is a great mistake to suppose that these are the only means to promote morality. Every truly civilizing influence is also a reforming one. By this we do not mean that miscalled civilization which multiplies wants, and increases luxury and develops refinement in a few, at the expense of the many, but that advancement of mind and of knowledge, which is forever disclosing better methods of living and diffusing them among the whole people. Dr. Howard Crosby, president of the Society for the Prevention of Crime, in New York, and who has had wide opportunities of observing the condition of morality in that city, has recently declared that the moral condition of New York has vastly improved during the past few years, and that fifty years ago, although there was far less of the foreign element than there is now, a low condition of morality existed that would not be tolerated at the present time. What is true of New York in this respect is equally true of our other cities, and if there be any pessimist who points to the well-known corruptions and vices which still exist as a refutation of this statement, we would remind him that the very fact that such things are now brought to the light, discussed, and condemned, is a proof that they are on the decline. When a community is deeply sunk in immorality, little or no comment is made on the fact. When we come to seek into the causes of this improvement, we shall find that among the most prominent are the practical results of scientific progress and the civilizing tendencies of the age. There is no question that dirt, disease, and darkness are prevalent sources of vice and crime, and whatever influences are brought to bear against them will also press heavily against immorality. The increasing value set upon health, as shown alike in sanitary laws and regulations and in the greater willingness manifested by the community to understand and adopt hygienic modes of life, is beyond dispute. The improvements in house building and drainage; the introduction of water, pure and plentiful; the freer admission of fresh air; the better systems of ventilation; the brilliant lighting up of our city streets—all contribute to the prevention of crime and to the spread of a higher type of morality, while increasing the health, peace, and comfort of the community. And when to all these we add the better and wider education given to the rising generation than was thought possible fifty years ago, we shall find abundant reason for the moral advancement which has been made. There are some persons who feel quite powerless to help on the cause of reform, or to improve the moral character of a single individual, because they have no gift for influencing men by direct appeal. They have, perhaps, tried and failed, and so, although they would like to do some good in the world, they are hopeless of any success. Let such take courage as they remember how many indirect, yet most effectual, methods there are of accomplishing this end. Let them look over the multitudes of civilizing agencies that are silently working in the interests of morality, and attach themselves to such as most heartily engage their interest. Every intelligent individual must be in sympathy with some of them; and it is just there that his services are needed and will be most valuable. Nor let him make the mistake of supposing that he is thus working upon a lower or inferior plane. It is in works of benevolence and reform, just as in all other kinds of work—that which a man can do best is the very best thing for him to do. So, if one man is interested in sanitary schemes and another in evening schools; if one is anxious for free libraries and another for free parks; if one can help to secure good roads and clean streets and another can aid in protecting children or dumb animals from ill-treatment, let each be assured that in such exertions he is doing his share in promoting morality and in elevating character as surely and as effectually as those whose peculiar province it is to teach or to preach, to admonish or to advise."

If the butcher's trade begets in him, the butcher, a disposition to use the knife more indiscriminately, and causes him to look upon the taking of life indifferently and unconcernedly, so that in a majority of the States he is disqualified from sitting upon a murderer's jury, there then must be something not only in the associations we keep but in the business we follow.

The average lawyer tries by every known means to clear his client. In 50% of the cases handled by 50% of the attorneys their clients are guilty and they know it. They do not break the law of their State or country simply because the laws in the main are made to screen the evil-doers and not the honest citizen. But how they can do this and affiliate with any one of the 1,100 different faiths, or attend their church organizations or services sincerely, is more than we can surmise. In contrast, however, we must mention an isolated case that has reached us well authenticated. A very prominent and able lawyer of New York City, who had the reputation of never losing a case, was accosted by a well-known offender of the law on trial for felony before the court of Oyer and Terminer. The attorney invited the would-be client into his private office and had him state his case. He finished, and the lawyer remarked, "You are guilty." "Well, I know that," replied the culprit, "that is why I want your services—you never lose a case." "Sir," said the lawyer, "you have come to the wrong office. I have never failed in any case before the courts; I account for it from the fact that I have never espoused a cause where I knew the client was guilty. Knowing I was right, I have thrown my whole soul into it, and won."

Gossip.—There is a vast deal of unhappiness in this world caused by gossip. Dr. J. G. Holland presents helpful ideas in the following:—

"What is the cure for gossip?—Simply culture. There is a great deal of gossip that has no malignity in it. Good-natured people talk about their neighbors because they have nothing else to talk about. As we write, there comes to us the picture of a family of young ladies. We have seen them at home, we have met them in galleries of art, we have caught glimpses of them going from a book store or library with a fresh volume in their hands. When we meet them they are full of what they have seen and read. They are brimming with questions. One topic of conversation is dropped only to give place to another in which they are interested. We have left them after a delightful hour, stimulated and refreshed, and during the whole hour not a neighbor's garment was soiled by so much as a touch. They had something to talk about. They knew something, and wanted to know more. They could listen as well as they could talk. To speak freely of a neighbor's doings and belongings would have seemed an impertinence to them, and, of course, an impropriety. They had no temptation to gossip, because the doings of their neighbors formed a subject very much less interesting than those which grew out of their knowledge and their culture.

"And this tells the whole story. The confirmed gossip is always either malicious or ignorant. The one variety needs a change of heart and the other a change of pasture. Gossip is always a personal confession either of malice or imbecility, and the young should not only shun it, but, by most thorough culture, relieve themselves from all temptation to indulge in it. It is a low, frivolous, and, too often, a dirty business. There are neighborhoods in which it rages like a pest. Churches are split in pieces by it. Neighbors are made enemies by it for life. In many persons it degenerates into a chronic disease, which is practically incurable. Let the young cure it while they may."

MARRIED LIFE.—As the family is the center about which all life revolves, it is absolutely essential to have happy relations there. Husbands too often neglect their wives and homes. "Women are lonely," says Mrs. Annie Jenness. "They miss their husbands. What amount of companionship exists between the American woman and the man? He starts for his office as soon as his breakfast is hurriedly swallowed. He does not come home at the lunch hour. He is barely in season for a late dinner. Very possibly he belongs to a club and has an engagement as soon as dinner is done.

"If not that, his head is in bank or counting-house, and he studies the stock quotations in the night's paper, and counts, as against a possible rise of wheat, the day's gossip, with which his wife is overflowing, very small potatoes. They have callers, or they go to opera or theater. It may easily happen that they do not spend ten minutes in conversation with each other during the day. American men are always in a hurry. They seem to live for the sole purpose of catching trains. They have no time to amuse or be amused.

"The conditions of modern life separate them from women. The lives of men grow more and more simple—business comprehends the whole. The lives of women grow more and more complex—everything which is not business is given over to them. A man past the romantic epoch, who honestly enjoys talking with women, is not an average mortal. The every-day sort of man takes pains to be detained somewhere until all the guests have departed from his wife's 5 o'clock tea. The couple live in different worlds. The world is now discussing why marriage is a failure, if it is? Then consider this collection of reasons:—

"When either of the parties marry for money.

"When the lord of creation pays more for cigars than his better half does for hosiery, boots, and bonnets.

"When one of the parties engages in a business that is not approved by the other.

"When both parties persist in arguing over a subject upon which they never have and never can think alike.

"When neither husband nor wife takes a vacation.

"When the vacations are taken by one side of the house only.

"When a man attempts to tell his wife what style of bonnet she must wear.

"When a man's Christmas presents to his wife consist of boot-jacks, shirts, and gloves for himself.

"When the watchword is, 'Each for himself.'

"When dinner is not ready at dinner-time.

"When 'he' snores his loudest while 'she' kindles the fire.

"When 'father' takes half of the pie and leaves the other half for the one that made it and her eight children.

"When the children are given the neck and back of the chicken.

"When children are obliged to clamor for their rights.

"When the money that should go for a book goes for what only one side of the house knows anything about.

"When there is too much latch-key.

"When politeness, fine manners, and kindly attentions are reserved for company or visits abroad."

CHAPTER XIII.

"The greatest friend of truth is time."

WHAT WE INHERIT FROM THE PAST.

The world moves only through the constant accumulation and conservation of force—the force of mind. We are not capable of conceiving the immense wastage of this force from year to year and from century to century. If we produce a great inventor we are ignorantly proud of him. We wonder at him as if he were a miracle. A great thinker in mechanics, in art, in science, in letters, astonishes as if he were a prodigy, when he is really only an approach to what all men have the right to be, to what all men may become when the right mind has applied to it the right compelling power of suggestion from the force of other minds. As surely as the plant is involved in its seed, so surely is all the progress of the future involved in the thought of the past, recorded in books as far as it is possible to record it at all. The telephone, the telegraph, the phonograph, the steam-engine, the power loom —every result of the application of mind in the subjection of matter— existed in the minds of men and was recorded in books years before the thought gave suggestion to the mind which applied it practically. Back of the mind of the great thinker in poetry, in statesmanship, in science, in mechanics, is the conserved force of the minds preceding him. But what does it all avail if it is wasted? We may have now a thousand Edisons, Fultons, Morses and Maurys, inert and practically useless because of force unapplied that might set them in motion to make the lives of millions, born and unborn, easier and happier. We have poets, statesmen, scientists, and inventors as unknown and unproductive as the worms which change them into productive forms of matter in country church-yards, where some Gray finds them and touches us with a sense of their loss to us without suggesting the remedy. What remedy is there if it is not this of making the suggested possibility of the past the endeavor of the present and the achievement of the future? How is that possible, if we regard our capable men as miracles, when our own incapacity to understand is the only miracle when we leave the great possibilities of mind in unnumbered "thousands to die with the matter of their bodies? Charity builds a small-pox hospital and men bless it —rightly. It benefits its hundreds and its thousands. The same benevolence, operating under the force of the conserved energy of mind, discovers vaccination, and so benefits millions and tens of millions for ages after the small-pox hospital is back in the clay from which its bricks were burned. There is here no parallel possible between the results achieved—those of the one hand so immensely exceed those of the other. The whole problem of the present and future is to bring the accumulated force of suggestion from the past to bear on the given point—on the mind of the living man, capable in possibility, and failing to achieve only for lack of stimulus—of force, of power—as a steam-engine is incapable without force applied from without. And as it is the last shovel of coal that sets the engine to work, so the mind, prepared for the final suggestion that is to give it its highest usefulness, will remain inert if the suggestion fails it. These suggestions may come from nature or directly from other minds, but in the main they come from the force of mind preserved in books. Can there be any greater, any more capable benevolence, than that which gives this force its widest possible application? A million dollars may endow a hospital for a century. Half as much in an endowment making a library free may bring pressure to bear on some brain, that, as a result, will save more suffering for the human race than has been saved by vaccination."

CHAPTER XIV.

LONGEVITY.

"Tell me not in mournful numbers,
   Life is but an empty dream,
For the soul is dead that slumbers,
   And things are not what they seem."

   How long shall a man live? That depends entirely upon the *Liver!*— *Punch.*

If you have read with care the preceding chapters of this work, and paused between the lines to reflect, you will not now have to be retold our panacea for a long life. By this we mean the usually allotted three-score and ten, or also the 120 years given as the limit in Genesis, 3rd and 6th chapters. These ages, however, are not common in any country or age. There are many instances of 70 years, but not enough to be called common, while it is the "survival of the fittest" that reach 120 years.

In the United States only 5.6% of population are above 60 years and probably not more than 4-1/2% are over 70 years. Norway has the best record, with 9% of the population above the age of 60. Japan has 1,182,000 people over 70 years, but only 73 of these are over 100, and 1 alone has reached the age of 111 years. Probably the oldest human being living in the United States at this writing is the old Indian named Gabriel, residing at or near Castroville, Cal., 100 miles south of San Francisco. He has an authentic history of 146 years, and he is believed to be over 150 years old. But for real characteristic longevity, we must visit the mountain fastnesses of Thibet, in Asia, where live a number of specimens of the human family that have a recorded history back to the latter part of the 16th century.

We have previously told you that by regularity alone man may reach the age of 100 years. Now we intend to treat more the possibilities of how long it is possible for mankind to retain all their mental faculties and enjoy sufficient vital force to battle with the world for a livelihood. We are led to believe, like Dr. Wm. A. Hammond, a prominent physician of New York City "that there is no physiological reason at the present day why man should die." (Further on we give more of the Doctor's theory.) Just so long, however, as there are no paid teachers to show how not to get sick, how to keep the physique and mind from tiring, the heart from growing weary and discontented, just so long will the average of life remain under 40 years and the grave-yards continue to be populated. There are hundreds of reasons why this or that clan or sect live longer than the other sect or clan, but what we wish to convey is that none of them live out all their days. For instance, in comparison with other nations not mentioned, the German can drink more beer, the Frenchman more wine, the Russian more pure spirits, the Englishman more brandy, and the American more whisky, before harm is perceptible, likewise the Chinese can smoke more opium and the Russian a stronger cigarette, and more of them, before harm is apparent to others. No matter what an individual's creed, color, or nationality, if he be intelligent and clearly endowed with the five known senses, he does know that any narcotic, no matter of what nature, even if it is as mild as steeped tea leaves and as odorless as pure water, is a detriment to some one of the senses. As each sense is dulled, the others must sympathize with it; so it will not require an instrument to measure to the .001 part of an inch, or to a single vibration of the violet ray, to test the degree of injury that the human structure received for each variation from the path of perfection.

If perfection of climate is sought, perfect sanitation obtained, regularity, cleanliness, uprightness, temperance, and self-control practiced, if the bodily waste is supplied with nature's fruits, grains, vegetables, and herbs, if drinking is done at nature's fountain for thirst, life will be prolonged to see the light in more than one century. Finally, add to that, if self is forgotten, and only the comfort of others remembered and regarded, life may be indefinitely prolonged.

M. Chevreul, the eminent French scientist, died April 9, 1889, aged 103 years. "On the 31st day of August, 1886, he attained the age of 100 years, and was still in vigorous health, and with all his faculties unimpaired. The occasion 'was celebrated by the students of Paris, among whom he is a great favorite, and by the French people generally, with enthusiasm.' The Paris *Journal Illustre* seized upon the opportunity to interview him in a manner that is described as marking 'an era in this line of journalistic enterprise. Not only were his words taken down *verbatim*, but his various attitudes while speaking were photographed by the instantaneous process, and engraved,' twelve illustrations being given in the interview. M. Chevreul is an important figure in the scientific world, and the interview contains many useful lessons in hygiene and philosophy, not the least of which is described by his interviewer as an exposition of the 'chemical secret of longevity.' In a condensed form, it is as follows: He regards longevity as a great blessing, and declares that the method by which it may be secured is easy to learn; but I think that with many people it would be difficult to follow. He laid down the proposition that the larger proportion of the human race die of disease and not of old age. Now, he finds that while we should especially guard against drawing general conclusions from particular cases, yet it is nevertheless true that the study of particular cases may and should conduct us to general precepts. It is necessary for each one to study his personal aptitudes, and conform to them with a constant firmness. Every *régime* is personal, and 'I cannot too much insist upon this essential point, that what is suitable for one may not be for another. It is, then, important for each one to note well what is adapted to his own constitution. Thus, I have the same aversion to fish as to fermented liquors, especially to wine, also a distaste for a large number of vegetables, and I could never drink milk. Shall I conclude, then, that fish, that the vegetables which I do not relish, and milk, are not nutritive?—Certainly not; for I judge by a general rule and not by my own idiosyncrasies. Coffee and chocolate agree with me; the latter is especially nutritive, and gives me an appetite for food. It is for me an aperient. Shall I conclude from this that chocolate would give everybody an appetite?'

"He maintains a barometric exactness and regularity in all the habits of his daily life,—eats at fixed hours, takes his time, and leaves the table with some appetite for more. He says he remembers the words of the wise man, 'The stomach has slain more men than war,' and that the Spartans proscribed those citizens who were too fat.

"I use little salt or spices, and but little coffee, and I flee as from a pest from all those excitants of which I feel no need, and from all tobacco and alcoholics in whatever form they may present themselves.'

"He divides his day, the morning to exact science, the middle of the day to philosophy, and the evening to music and poetry. 'But above all, no discussion at the table. One should only eat with a calm spirit. Let the dining-room remain the dining-room, and never be turned into a room for argument. Discussion while eating is a cushion of needles in the stomach.'"

Dr. Felix L. Oswald has made the following brilliant conclusions in the "Curiosities of Longevity:"—

"Among the centenarians of all nations and all times, a significant plurality were either rustics, or city dwellers addicted to outdoor pursuits. Centenarians are remarkably frequent among the bailiff-ridden boors of Southern Russia, and the five oldest persons of modern times were care-worn if not abjectly poor villagers: Peter Czartan, who died in a hamlet near Belgrade, 1724, in his *hundred and eighty-fifth year*; the Russian beggar Kamartzik, a native of Polotzk, who reached an age of one hundred and sixty-three years, and died in consequence of an accident; the fisherman Jenkins, who, in spite of life-long penury, lived at least a century and a half (the estimate of his neighbors varying from one hundred and fifty-eight to one hundred and sixty-nine years); the negress Truxo, who died in slavery on the plantation of a Tucuman physician, in her hundred and seventy-fifth year; and the day-laborer, Thomas Parr, who attained the pretty-well-authenticated age of one hundred and fifty-two years, and who died a few weeks after his removal from country air and indigence to comfort and city quarters. If dietetic restrictions tend to prolong human life, the rule would seem to be chiefly confirmed by its exceptions. The children of Israel are apt to ascribe their certainly remarkable longevity to the Mosaic interdict of hogs' flesh....

"John H. Brown, M. D., the Berwick Æsculapius, enumerates a long list of patients who had postponed their funeral by following his plan of systematic hygiene—the plan, namely, of 'toning down' plethora by bleeding and cathartics, and of 'toning up' debility by means of beef and brandy. But sixteen hundred years ago the philosopher Lucian called attention to the exceptional longevity of the Pythagorean ascetics, whose religious by-laws enjoined total abstinence from wine and all sorts of animal food. The naturalist Brehm describes the robust physique of a Soudan chieftain who, at the reputed age of one hundred and six years, could hurl a stone with force sufficient to kill a jackal at a distance of fifty yards, and thought nothing of starving for a week or two if his foragers happened to return empty-handed. But the same traveler mentions that his swarthy Nestor now and then compensated such fasts by barbecues lasting from ten to twenty-four hours, and including a *mélange* of marrow-fat and pepper-grass, besides dozens of hard-boiled crane's eggs, jerboa stew, and deep draughts of clarified butter. Long fasts certainly enhance the vigor of the digestive organs, but the net result of repeating such experiments seems rather difficult to reconcile with the experience of Luigi Cornaro, the Venetian reformer, who managed to outlive all his cousins and schoolmates, and ascribed his success to the mathematical regularity of his bill of fare, which, during the last sixty years of his self-denying existence, had been limited to twelve ounces of solid food and fourteen ounces of fluids—wine chiefly, a beverage which the Soudanese emir would have rejected with a snort of virtuous horror. Dr. Virchow, though by no means an advocate of total abstinence, admits that the longevity of the Semitic desert-dwellers can be explained only by their caution in the use of stimulants—a virtue which in their case would, indeed, appear to offset an unusual number of circumstantial disadvantages—thirst, fiery suns, and fiery passions being decidedly unpropitious to length of life.

"And here, at last, we may strike a bit of *terra firma* in the quicksands of speculative hygiene. 'Take a hundred different animals,' says the sanitarian Schrodt, and you will find them to prefer a hundred different sorts of solid food, but they all drink milk in infancy, and afterward water; and considering the infinite variety of comestibles a healthy human stomach contrives to digest, we might very well agree to deserve that privilege by limiting the variety of our beverages.' Instinct certainly abhors the first taste of alcoholic liquors, and statistics prove that in all climes and among all nations the disease-resisting power of the human organism is diminished by the habitual use of toxic stimulants. Mohammed, Buddha, and Zoroaster agree on that point, and the esoteric teachings of Pythagoras may have qualified his rather fanciful objections to grape-juice by the practical hope of longevity. A complete list of infallible prescriptions for the prolongation of human life would fill a voluminous book, and would include some decidedly curious specifics. 'To what do you ascribe your hale old age?' the Emperor Augustus asked a centenarian whom he found wrestling in the *palæstra* and bandying jokes with the young athletes. '*Intus mulso, foris oleo*,' said the old fellow—'Oil for the skin and mead [water and honey] for the inner man.' Cardanus suggests that old age might be indefinitely postponed by a semi-fluid diet warmed (like mothers' milk) to the exact temperature of the human system and Voltaire accuses his rival Maupertuis of having hoped to attain a similar result by varnishing his hide with a sort of resinous paint (*un poix résineux*) that would prevent the vital strength from evaporating by exhalation. Robert Burton recommends 'oil of unaphar and dormouse fat;' Paracelsus, rectified spirits of alcohol; Horace, olives and marsh-mallows. Dr. Zimmerman, the medical adviser of Frederick the Great, sums up the 'Art of Longevity' in the following words: 'Temperate habits, outdoor exercise, and steady industry, sweetened by occasional festivals.'"

"The increasing longevity of man is attracting considerable attention from collectors of statistics, and some curious facts are being elicited. According to the last census, 10 per cent of the people who died between 1870 and 1880 had outlived the traditional three-score years and ten, whereas of the deaths between 1840 and 1850, only 7.47 per cent were of persons of that age. In 1850, 16.90 per cent of the deaths were of children under one year of age; in 1880, the proportion was 23.24, showing a smaller percentage of deaths among adults. The average length of life in England 300 years ago was only twenty years. In France the average length of life, under Louis XVIII., was twenty-eight years. Actuaries are figuring that within the past half-century the average length of life has greatly increased."

"A study of this subject is impeded by the tendency of almost everyone to generalize from individual examples within his own observation. This is almost sure to be misleading, because no one's acquaintance is so large that it embraces factors enough to base a theory on. People say that life is longer than it used to be, because Palmerston rode to hounds at 82, and Peter Cooper and the Emperor William were intellectually vigorous at over 91. They forget that Marino Faliero was over 80 when he concocted his plot, and that the blind Dodge Dandolo was 84 when he took Constantinople. Every age has produced a few long-lived men, and here and there a centenarian."

"The question of importance is not whether this age is yielding more centenarians than former ages, but whether, on the average, the age of man is longer than it was, and if so, how much longer? The grounds for an increased longevity—better doctors and more of them, better drainage, more wholesome food, wiser habits, and better facilities for securing change of air—justify the belief that life is lengthening, to what degree it is hard to say. M. Flourens, who had made a life study of the subject, said that every man ought to live to be a hundred, if he took care of himself."

"In a number of the *Popular Science Monthly* is an article by Clement Milton Hammond on the prolongation of human life that is interesting both in the way of being readable and as based on returns as to an unusually large number of persons above eighty years of age. The facts were obtained by sending out 5,000 blanks to be filled. They were sent through New England only and were intended to cover personal history and hereditary influence. Over 3,500 of the blanks were filled out and returned. They show that less than 5 per cent remained unmarried through life, the unmarried women being three times as numerous as the unmarried men. The average number of children was five. Five out of six of the old people had light complexions, blue or gray eyes, and abundant brown hair. The men were generally tall and ranged in weight from 100 to 160 pounds, with a few of 200 pounds, and the women of medium size, weighing from 100 to 120 pounds, with some exceptional cases up to 180 pounds. The men were generally bony and muscular, and the women the opposite. At the time of record the hair was generally thick, the teeth poor or entirely gone, the skin only slightly wrinkled. Generally their habits of eating and sleeping have been conspicuously regular. They have as a rule adhered to one occupation through life, and of the 1,000 men 461 were farmers. Few have used alcoholic drink stronger than cider. A large majority of the men used tobacco. The average age of the parents and grandparents of the persons reported on was about sixty-five. The average time of sleep was about eight hours."

Dr. Maurice advances some staunch ideas on old age:—

"Do poor people live longer than the affluent? There are so many more poor in the world than there are rich that we can be sure of finding more poor old people. Probably excessive wealth is a burden sure to exhaust its possessor in the care of it. Our millionaires, however, are men for the most part who began poor and were possessed of tenacious vitality, that is, with a grip on other things as strong as on the money bags. Professor Humphrey's 'Report on Age of Persons' gives us 824 persons, of both sexes, of whom about half were poor and the rest at least in good circumstances, 10 per cent only being possessed of wealth. The real truth seems to be that poverty, with an iron constitution and sound nerves, is most likely to produce an instance of extreme age; but the possession of the comforts and amenities of life produces by far the best average of ages. The average age of the middle classes has always surpassed that of others; but at present sanitation forces on the poor so many provisions against disease that they are saved from their former high death-rate, and brought quite near the privately better-bred and furnished class.

"There has certainly been long sustained, in proverbs and otherwise, a conviction that early rising and early retiring have much to do with prolonged vitality. Franklin insisted on it vigorously. Lord Mansfield, also, held it to be an important item in his sustained vigor to near ninety. I am inclined to believe that the estimate is not erroneous. We are far more the creatures of habit than we generally allow. At certain moments we become regularly hungry, regularly sleepy, and so with all other functions. It is wise beyond doubt to recognize this fact and never break our habits, that is, our useful habits. But beyond this, there are certain habits dependent on cosmical causes, such as movements of the sun. Our natural rest would seem to be properly conformed, in the main, to the appearance and disappearance of daylight.

"But after we have fairly and fully considered the subject, there remains the one fact that idleness will end life sooner than any other cause. The hour that any person retires from any and all occupation he is sure to drop into decadence. The mind is very sure to begin to lose its clearness when it is withdrawn from regular exercise. Both brain and muscular power lapse with lack of activity. The custom of working excessively till sixty-five or seventy, and then withdrawing from business, is wrong at both ends. We crowd life at the beginning, and let its functioning grow torpid at the close. Much is lost to age by our modern methods of locomotion. Great walkers are scarce; there is almost a total lack of horse-back exercise. Carriage-riding over smooth roads in no way compensates."

Perhaps there is nothing that prolongs life more than genial, hearty *laughter*. William Matthews says "that there is not a remote corner or little inlet of the minute blood-vessels of the human body that does not feel some wavelet from the great convulsion caused by hearty laughter shaking the central man. Not only does the blood move more quickly than it is wont, but its chemical or electric condition is distinctly modified, and it conveys a different impression to the organs of the body, as it visits them on that particular mystic journey when the man laughs, from what it does at other times. A genial, hearty laugh, therefore, prolongs life, by conveying a distinct and additional stimulus to the vital forces. Best of all, it has no remorse in it. It leaves no sting, except in the sides, and that goes off. Cicero thought so highly of it that he complained bitterly at one time that his fellow-citizens had all forgotten to laugh: *Civem mehercule non puto esse qui his temporibus ridere possit*. Titus, the Roman emperor, thought he had lost a day if he had passed it without laughing. What a world would this be without laughter! To what a dreary, dismal complexion should we all come at last, were all fun and cachination expurged from our solemn and scientific planet! Care would soon overwhelm us; the heart would corrode; the river of life would be like the lake of the Dismal Swamp; we should begin our career with a sigh, and end it with a groan; while cadaverous faces, and words to the tune of 'The Dead March in Saul,' would make up the whole interlude of our existence."

"Hume, the historian, in examining a French manuscript containing accounts of some private disbursements of King Edward II. of England, found, among others, one item of a crown paid to somebody for making the king laugh. Could one conceive of a wiser investment? Perhaps by paying one crown Edward saved another. 'The most utterly lost of all days,' says Chamfort, 'is that on which you have not once laughed.' Even that grimmest and most saturnine of men, who, though he made others roar with merriment, was never known to smile, and who died 'in a rage, like a poisoned rat in a hole'—Dean Swift—has called laughter 'the most innocent of all diuretics.' Yet the philosopher of Concord, R. W. Emerson, is reported as having said in a lecture: 'Laughter is to be avoided. Lord Chesterfield said that after he had come to the years of understanding he never laughed.' Lord Chesterfield would have had far more influence if, instead of repressing every inclination to laugh, he had now and then given his ribs a holiday—nay, if he had even roared outright; for it would have disabused the public of the notion that he never obeyed a natural impulse, but that everything he said and did was prestudied—done by square, rule, and compass. As it was, though he was confessedly the politest, best-bred, most insinuating man at court, yet he was regularly and invariably out-flanked and out-maneuvered by Sir Robert Walpole, who had the heartiest laugh in the kingdom, and by the Duke of Newcastle, who had the worst manners in the world. In commending laughter, we mean genuine laughter, not a make-believe, not the artificial or falsetto laugh of fashionable society, nor, again, the mere smile of acquiescent politeness, or the crackling of thorns under a pot, or the curl of the lips that indicates in the laughter a belief in his fancied superiority. Still less do we mean the hollow, mocking laugh of the cynic. The laughter which we would commend as healthful is not bitter, but kindly, genial, and sympathetic."

No Physiological Reason for Death.—"Dr. William A. Hammond, a prominent physician of New York, who has written several medical treatises, and was some years ago Surgeon-General of the United States Army, has recently set forth his belief that there is no physiological reason at the present day why man should die. He maintains that people die through the ignorance of the laws which govern their existence, and from their inability, or indisposition, to attend to those laws with which they are acquainted. Now, as the business of medical men has ostensibly been for the last four thousand years to prolong human life, and as Dr. Hammond affirms that there is no good reason why people should die, the wonder is why men of his school have not drawn up some formula by which they could live on for three or four thousand years, at least. There has always been a vague impression that the knowledge of the preservation of human life had been lost, and that in some favored era of the world's history that knowledge would be recovered.

"If there is such a thing as a hidden law of life, which, when discovered and asserted, will arrest physical decay and prevent death, except by accident, Doctor Hammond, and all who hold to his doctrine, ought to lose no time in making it known. This medical authority reasons that, as the human body is constantly dying and constantly renewing its particles, this law of displacement and renewal ought to be perpetual, and that when it is discovered just what substances are best fitted to maintain this equipoise, as it were, there should be no giving out of the physical powers.

"'The food that man takes into his stomach,' says Doctor Hammond, 'ought to be of such quantity and quality as would exactly repair the losses which, through the action of the several organs, his body is to undergo. If it is excessive in either of these directions, or if it is deficient, disease of some kind will certainly be the result. If he knew enough to be able to adjust his daily food to the expected daily requirements of his system, disease could never ensue through the exhaustion of any one of his vital organs. A large majority of the morbid affections to which he is subject are due to a lack of this knowledge.

"'Now, suppose that he is exactly right in his calculations, and that the food taken is neither too great nor too little, but exactly compensates the anticipated losses, the death of each cell in the brain, or the heart, or the muscles, etc., will be followed by the birth of a new cell, which will take its place and assume its functions. Gout, rheumatism, liver and kidney diseases, heart affections, softening and other destructive disorders of the brain, the various morbid conditions to which the digestive organs are subject, would be impossible except through the action of some external force, such as the swallowing of sulphuric acid, or a blow on the head, or a stab with a knife, which would come clearly within the class of accidents, and of course many of these would be avoidable.'

"Dr. Hammond's theory supposes that the time will come when the individual will have learned the uttermost thing about the laws of life, and when he will conform so strictly to these laws that he will have nothing more to learn in regard to the best way of living. It may require ages for this progress, but when it is attained, and the race is set free from all morbific influences, physical death would be impossible. The summary of his points is that 'people die from ignorance of the laws of life; and from willfulness in not obeying the laws they know.' That may be a part of the truth which is very near the surface. But the other demonstration is not quite so clear as could be wished—that there can be any such thing as an eternity of physical life, even if all the laws touching that life were known and every one of them obeyed."

PART II - CHAPTER I.

DISEASES AND REMEDIES; HOW TO PREVENT MOST MALADIES AND CURE ILLS POSSESSED.

Note.—If the reader is in haste to know what will cure this or that trouble, before perusing the pages of this entire pamphlet, such as cramp, colic, indigestion, constipation, headache, etc., the index found in the back part of this work will give immediate reference, and the prescriptions instant relief. If you are cured thereby of any of the many maladies that beset the human family, remember that it is only temporary; for to be cured of any disease permanently requires the removal of the cause. One of the objects of this book is to convey that information.

The great disparity between the actions and teachings of many of our principal writers must be apparent to every reader of books, pamphlets, and editorials, upon the subject of health and its allies, happiness and longevity. Many of the leading exponents of temperance have periodical spells of drunkenness, and some drink all the time. The prominent articles written upon the subject of sanitary matters and cleanliness, are generally by the editor whose office is the scene of disorder, the floor covered with tobacco quids, old rubbish and dust, and the corners filled with cobwebs. The writer upon the subject of poverty and the wrongs of the poor, has his headquarters fitted up in the most magnificent style;—he never knew what it was to want for a meal, nor did he ever darken the door of real poverty. The missionary advocate soliciting funds for the heathen and down-trodden poor of foreign lands, more than likely never crossed the borders of his own State, certainly has not taken a stroll through the dark lanes and alleys, or climbed the dingy stairways of the tenement houses of his own city. If he had done so, a more effective appeal would have gone up for the suffering poor and spiritually blind of the principal unsanitary municipalities of his own country. The physician with a bad cough and broken-down constitution is still prescribing for consumptives and patients with all manner of aches and pains, of which his own body is a perfect index.

And the minister who has not yet lost all his hatred for "that other sect," and occasionally assists in persecuting it, is still teaching the doctrine of the meek and lowly Nazarene. Having experienced a large number of diseases and their successful remedies, we have for several years been collecting the most reliable data and testimony on many—in short most—of mankind's bodily ills. In this second part we present them for your benefit.

There are about 11,000 remedies mentioned in the 15th edition of the "United States Dispensatory," by reference to which it will be seen that each affliction to which flesh is heir must be more than well drugged. It is the fault of the community at large that the necessity of such a work exists. There is no demand for any form of disease even with the improper state of society as it is to-day. Extreme old age and a limited number of accidents are all that can be necessary to record. The following is an admirable article from the St. Louis *Globe Democrat,* which is quite pertinent.

"SANITATION AND SANITY.—The general subject of sanitation now covers our architecture and our home life; our sewerage and disposition of waste; our personal cleanliness and contact in all social relations; our food and drink, both as to quality and kind; quarantine and other preventives against contagion and infection; the purification of streams, and the cleansing of the air of smoke and foul vapors; in fact, the whole subject of health or wholeness. * * * A national board of health was as unthought of as was an Atlantic cable in 1800. But the fact that great epidemics were liable to invade us, and did invade us, led to a system of quarantine and to enforced vaccination. But the regulation by law of our social manners, so far as they bore on public health, was not undertaken to any extent until within the past decade. * * * Indeed, public sentiment is as yet so uninformed that thorough laws in the case could not be enacted or enforced. There is not a stream in the United States that can be kept entirely free from pollution. The sanitary value of this is not understood by even the intelligent populace. The drainage of swamps is neglected in the neighborhood of our larger cities."
"St. Louis has tolerated inside her limits pools that have made fevers of a malarious sort, with spinal meningitis, as common as croup. Chicago has acres of rotting vegetable matter inside the corporation every autumn. The inroads of yellow fever have always been invited by the unsanitary condition of Southern towns. The reports of Surgeon-General Hamilton, last summer, showed that the pest found its first welcome in a town where

sewerage was wholly neglected, and tons of rotting sawdust and refuse filled the heated air with fever conditions.

"The discovery of the germ origin of diphtheria and of the typhoid forms of fever, has led to great changes in thousands of households. Our houses are constructed with far more attention to ventilation and proper heating. We shall finally get rid of drunkenness and intemperance of other sorts, on sanitary grounds mainly. Alcohol has been considered as at least valuable in moderation. It has been looked upon as a medicine. That its value as a stimulant hangs on the previous abuse of health is now understood, and its value purely as a very temporary bridging of weakness alone is conceded. That the drink habit is in any sense, however moderate, of sanitary value, is disproved. Few doctors prescribe any form of alcohol for habitual use. The saloon is unsanitary in all its effects. The temperance issue rests at that point. Animals to which spirits have been given in their food digest nearly one-half less than other animals of the kind. The nutrition of the human body demands the abolition of stimulants and narcotics. The saloon will go ultimately as a nuisance to health. We have not yet reached a condition when public morals can rest on any other basis than health. It is doubtful if there can be a higher basis. What is unwholesome is wrong; what is promotive of health and completeness for the individual and for the community is right.

"Sanity is dependent on sanitary living. They both are derived etymologically from *sanitus*, and that from *sanus*, the Latin for sound or whole. Insanity has come to have the limited meaning of unsoundness of brain. * * * Insanity is on the increase in the United States, but not more so than nervous disorders in general. This indicates a tendency to a breakdown of the national type of organism, and cannot be considered with indifference. The fact exists as a consequence of the overwork and high pressure of modern life, but in this country is at its maximum, because, for several generations, we have been at white heat, subjecting a continent to our domestic purposes.

"The vast unfolding of means of wealth has also acted as a stimulant, compared to which alcohol is insignificant. Our lunatic asylums multiply, but are all full. The percentage of failure is greatest in California, where speculation has been most intense. It is impossible to avoid the problem.

How shall we reverse this tendency, and begin the construction of an American type of full, robust, conservative, and reserved energy? The underlying problem of all problems is to secure a constitution. A nation that lives and works in such a manner as to grow weaker in brain endurance and nerve power, and yet so lives that the demands on brain and nerves are increased, is doomed. The intensity of modern life is something we cannot reverse. We must adapt ourselves to it by securing larger and more systematic means of recuperation. Brain-workers must learn to use the first half of the day for work, and sacredly give the last half to rest and play. Night must be given back entirely to sleep. Withal it is clear that we must understand the close relation between sanity and sanitation. Our people can no longer eat and drink as grossly as our fathers did. The stomach gets not half the time it formerly did for digestion. It must, therefore, be delivered of half its toil. The introduction of stoves and modern conveniences must be accompanied by more rational ventilation. Active brains require a vast and regular supply of oxygen. It is not for the lungs alone that we need pure air, but for the brain. This is specifically an American problem, the readjustment of society, so that the mind shall be relieved of strain and consequent enfeeblement."

Individual, municipal, and national cleanliness by enactment of law are among the first steps that should be taken. The churches and schools should teach it as a prerequisite before godliness, or education in general; then with perfect ventilation, sanitation, and regularity of all the virtues, there will be no vices, and godliness and education will be contagious, just as though they were real diseases.

The first thing to undertake if you are desirous of freeing yourself of any disease, ache, or pain, is to stop the cause. Act on the same principle you would if you had a barrel that had leaked its contents and you desired to refill it,—first stop the leak. It is absolutely necessary that you study *cause* as well as *effect*, if you would know yourself.

THE SECRET OF SOUND HEALTH.—"Half the secret of life," says *MacMillan's Magazine*, "we are persuaded, is to know when we are grown old; and it is the half most hardly learned. It is more hardly learned, moreover, in the matter of exercise than in the matter of diet. There is no advice so commonly given to the ailing man of middle age as the advice to take more exercise, and there is perhaps none which leads him into so many pitfalls. This is particularly the case with the brain workers. The man who labors his brain must spare his body. He cannot burn the candle at both ends, and the attempt to do so will almost inevitably result in his lighting it in the middle to boot. Most men who use their brains much soon learn for themselves that the sense of physical exaltation, the glow of exuberant health which comes from a body strung to its full powers by continuous and severe exercise, is not favorable to study. The exercise such men need is the exercise that rests, not that which tires. They need to wash their brains with the fresh air of heaven, to bring into gentle play the muscles that have been lying idle while the head worked. Nor is it only to this class of laboring humanity that the advice to take exercise needs reservations. The time of violent delights soon passes, and the effort to protract it beyond its natural span is as dangerous as it is ridiculous. Some men, through nature or the accident of fortune, will, of course, be able to keep touch of it longer than others; but when once the touch has been lost, the struggle to regain it can add but sorrow to the labor. Of this our doctor makes a cardinal point; but, pertinent as his warning may be to the old, for whom, indeed, he has primarily compounded his *elixir vitæ*, it is yet more pertinent to men of middle age, and probably it is more necessary. It is in the latter period that most of the mischief is done. The old are commonly resigned to their lot; but few men will consent without a struggle to own that they are no longer young. All things are not good to all men, and all things are not always good to the same man. The man who confines his studies within one unchanging groove will hardly find his intellectual condition so light and nimble, so free of play, so capable of giving and receiving, as he who varies them according to his mood, for the mind needs rest and recreation no less than the body; it is not well to keep either always at high pressure. One fixed, unswerving system of diet, without regard to needs and seasons, or even to fancy, is not wise. The great secret of existence after all is to be the master and not the slave of both mind and body, and that is best done by giving both free rein within certain limits, which, as the old sages were universally agreed, each man must discover for himself. Happy are the words of Addison, and happily quoted: "A continual anxiety for life vitiates all the relishes of it, and casts a gloom over the whole face of nature, as it is impossible that we should take delight in anything that we are every moment afraid of losing. "One of the best methods of avoiding that pitiful anxiety is to learn within what limits we may safely indulge our desire for change, and then freely indulge it within them."

PART II - CHAPTER II.

We shall now take up a practical list of subjects, arranged in alphabetical order. Without any attempt at egotism, we claim that there are few nontechnical books extant that contain a superior selection of preventatives and remedies. Read carefully and judge for yourself. There are very few common or occasional afflictions which are not considered to some extent. Why always seek a doctor when you seem to be somewhat off your physical equilibrium? You will generally at each visit spend more money than this book will cost. Learn to provide against constant medical attention.

Accidents.—In sudden emergencies, either of accident or sickness, the first great requisite is presence of mind. Be calm. Endeavor, if possible, to grasp the situation, and do what is to be done promptly and quietly, until the arrival of the physician. All hurried and distracted motions, and all exciting noises, confuse the attendants and needlessly alarm the sufferer. In many cases, the course of immediate action is suggested by the circumstances; but where you do not know what aid to render, it is best to do nothing, except to make the patient as comfortable, for the time being, as possible. For all ordinary emergencies, ample directions are:—

"1. Always look in the direction in which you are moving.

"2. Never leave a car, or other public vehicle, when it is in motion.

"3. Never put your head or arms out of a vehicle when it is in motion.

"4. If a horse runs away with you, remain in the vehicle rather than risk the danger of jumping from it.

"5. In thunder-storms keep away from trees, metallic substances, doors, and windows. The lower part of a house is the safer.

"6. Never play with fire-arms. Always keep them beyond the reach of children.

"7. Avoid charcoal fumes; they are deadly when confined in a close room.

"8. Illuminating gas; be sure to turn it off. *Never blow it out.*

"9. When gas can be smelt in an apartment always air the room well before striking a match or bringing a light.

"10. When very cold, move quickly. If any part of the body is frozen, rub it with snow, and keep from the fire.

"11. Change wet clothing as soon as possible.

"12. Carefully avoid exposure to night air, in malarial districts.

"13. If necessary to go into an old vault or well, first introduce a burning candle. If the light burns low and finally goes out, carbonic acid gas is present and the place is unsafe to enter. Unslaked lime will absorb the gas and purify the air.

"14. Avoid walking on railroad tracks and icy sidewalks.

"15. When awake, very young children should never be left alone.

"16. Do not go, with loose hair or flowing garments, near dangerous machinery.

"17. Never touch gunpowder after dark.

"18. Never fondle a strange dog.

"19. Never light a fire with kerosene.

"20. Fill and trim your lamps in the day-time. Never trim or fill a lighted lamp.

"21. Keep matches in a closed metallic box.

"22. Have your horses rough-shod as soon as the ground freezes.

"23. When feeling dizzy or seasick, lie down.

"24. Do not close the damper of your stove too early. Better waste coal than run the risk of suffocation by gas.

"25. When climbing a ladder, look up and not down.

"26. In railroad traveling take the center of the car, and the middle car of the train, for safety.

"27. Eat only pure food, drink only pure liquids, think only pure thoughts, and keep your blood pure.

"28. In going through dry woods or over prairies do not smoke or cast matches about carelessly. There should be laws against this often wanton destruction of property.

"29. Look out for spontaneous ignition of oily rags, oil-painted canvas rolled up, wet iron filings.

"30. In entering mines not used, always try for gas before venturing into them.

"31. Do not be careless in any way whatever in connection with fire. The losses in the United States, in 1889, by fires as a result of carelessness amounted to nearly $100,000,000, while in San Francisco for the same year we find that fully 80% of the losses can be attributed to the same source."

Alcohol.—Felix L. Oswald, M.D., gives some very good ideas in *Good Health* on the alcoholic habit. "'Reform,' says an able political writer, 'is ever unpopular. All wrongs lie in the consent of the wronged, and what with the fierce support of those who thrive on the abuse, and the dull, heavy, ignorant conservatism of the masses, * * * it is a sad delusion to suppose that the cause is won when the argument is made.' An unquestionable preponderance of power, they argue, favors the side of the liquor venders, and in this world, at least, always finds a way to assert itself as right. The last link of that syllogism, however, is a rule with occasional exceptions. No unqualified evil has ever succeeded in maintaining its supremacy, and the evils of the alcohol vice are offset by no benefits. Alcohol has been called 'negative food,' because its physiological influence torpifies the functional energy of the digestive organs, and thus, for a time, renders the toper insensible to the cravings of hunger. The same effect, however, can be produced by a stunning blow, and we might as well claim that the interests of political economy could be promoted by a fierce war, because a knock-down stroke with the butt-end of a musket is apt to lessen the appetite of the afflicted soldier. No real benefit can result from the lethargizing effect of a poison dose, the retardation of the digestive functions being in every case a morbid and abnormal process, avenging its repetition by the fatty degeneration of the tissues and the impoverished condition of the blood. * * * During the horrible flood which a few months ago devastated the two richest provinces of the Chinese Empire, a number of vile marauders eked out an existence by fishing out wreckage and plundering floating corpses. The idea of mentioning the profits of these wretches as a compensating offset to the horrors of a public calamity would justly consign its propounder to the custody of a lunatic commission. Yet, by an exactly analogous line of argument, many of our political economists continue to defend the legal sanction of the liquor traffic. Nay, it might be seriously questioned if the total loss (by fire or water) of a billion bushels of grain would not be financially and morally preferable to their conversion into a life-blighting poison. According to the statistics of the Treasury Department, the alcohol drinkers of the United States (representing hardly one-fifth of the alcoholized nations of Christendom) spent during the last ten years a yearly average of $370,000,000 for whisky, $58,000,000 for other distilled liquors, $56,000,000 for wine, and $140,000,000 for ale and beer; together, $624,000,000 a year. That enormous sum has been far worse than wasted. It has been invested in the purchase of disease. It has been devoted to the development of idiocy, crime, and pauperism. It has turned blessings into a concentration of curses. The general recognition of these facts will seal the doom of the liquor traffic."

Dr. C. E. Spitka expresses some results of science investigating strong drinks:—

"Alcoholism among the ancients was therefore mainly or exclusively known in its acute phases, the drunken frenzy in which Alexander the Great killed Clitus being a familiar example. With the introduction of tobacco and playing cards, the saloon, the cellar-dive, and the bar-room usurped the place formerly held by the inn. The enlargement of cities deprived their inhabitants of rustic sports, and led to their seeking in other and more dangerous channels an escape from mental and physical strain, and a variation of routine monotony. It is generally conceded by those medical writers who are unshackled by prejudice that a certain amount of alcohol can be ingested with perfect impunity. That amount has been accurately determined by Dujardin-Beaumetz in the course of experiments made in the abattoirs of Paris. Transferring the result of his experiments to the human species, he concluded that a man weighing 120 pounds could take the equivalent of two ounces of alcohol a day for years without injury to any organ of the body. But when the amount taken daily exceeds the toleration-point, prolonged abuse is followed by results which are as sinister as they are insidious. In the dead-house of the Philadelphia Hospital, Formad found that, of 250 chronic alcoholists, nearly 99 per cent had fatty degeneration of the liver, 60 per cent had congestion or a dropsical state of the brain, the same proportion an inflamed or degenerated stomach, while not quite 1 per cent had normal kidneys. Of 17 children of drunken fathers observed by Voisin, 3 were idiots, 2 confirmed epileptics, 1 suffered from a congenital spinal disease, and the remainder died in early life with convulsions. Of 11 children similarly descended, cited by Dagonet, 9 died in the same way. Of 117 such births recorded in Alsace-Lorraine, 13 were still-born and 39 died of convulsive disorders shortly after birth. One drunken father had 7 still-born children in succession; another lost 8 of 12 by convulsions. It is not alone as a direct result of inebriety that a defective nervous system is thus transmitted. Even in his sober intervals, he whose nervous system has been shattered by alcohol is liable to have a degenerate or diseased offspring. Of 18 children recorded as born under these circumstances, Voisin found 8 epileptic and 10 idiotic. As if to prove beyond the possibility of a doubt that such degeneracy is due to the alcoholism of the parent, and to that alone, two French investigators, Mairet and Combemale, performed a series of experiments on dogs, by which they showed that the same result which the chronic inebriate is accused of producing in his offspring, through selfish indulgence, can be produced at will in the offspring of lower animals by compulsory induction of the same vice in them."

An English investigation, just completed, puts in tangible form the effect of the use of alcohol, from observations covering 4,234 cases in all walks of life. This report shows that, with men over twenty-five, the intemperate use of alcohol cuts off ten years from life, those who never drink to excess, or use no liquor, living, on the average, ten years longer than those who do. Indulgence, if carried to excess, doubles diseases of the liver, quadruples those of the kidneys, and greatly increases the number of deaths from pneumonia, pleurisy, and epilepsy.

It is not often appreciated how many people die annually from the effects of strong drink. Dr. Norman Kerr, an eminent physician of England, believing the statement of temperance people to be extravagant, that 60,000 people die annually from the effects of strong drink, began as early as 1870 a personal inquiry, in connection with several medical men and experts, expecting to quickly disprove the same. According to their deductions, the latest estimates of deaths of adults annually caused through intemperance is, in Great Britain, 120,000; in France, 142,000; in the United States, 80,000 —or nearly a half million each year in three countries aggregating a population of 112,000,000.

Excessive Beer Drinking.—In the earlier part of our work we endeavored to impress on our readers the necessity of regularity and the avoidance of excesses. The last week of 1889 in New York City saw two prominent brewers buried, and two others of the guild were near death. None of them were, or are, over forty-seven years old. Kidney and heart disease were the causes of death in the case of the first two. Similar ailments have marked the other two gentlemen for the grave. The question arises, Was it beer or champagne that caused these diseases? In this connection the statement a physician of Bellevue Hospital once made is not amiss. These are his words: "The worst cases of alcoholic ailments coming under our observation are those resulting from excessive beer drinking."

In appearance the beer drinker may be the picture of health; but in reality he is most incapable of resisting disease. A slight injury, a severe cold, or a shock to the body or mind, will commonly provoke acute disease, ending fatally. Compared with other inebriates who use different kinds of alcohol, he is more incurable and more generally diseased. It is our observation that beer drinking in this country produces the very lowest kind of inebriety, closely allied to criminal insanity. The most dangerous class of ruffians in our large cities are beer drinkers. Intellectually, a stupor amounting almost to paralysis arrests the reason, changing all the higher faculties into a mere animalism, sensual, selfish, sluggish, varied only with paroxysms of anger, senseless and brutal.

That men are the sex most addicted to stimulating but injurious habits is sadly growing less true, and women are finding recourse too often to poisonous invigorators. If one-half of what the doctors are saying all over the country is true, there may soon be a greater need of a temperance reform among the women than there ever has been among the men. Strong drink, however, is not the monster by which the women may be enslaved, but a strong and poisonous drug equally baneful in its effect.

This drug is antipyrine. It is a white powder, slightly bitter, and soluble in water. Until about a year ago it was prescribed for fevers only, but a French medical college recommended it for headaches and other pains and disorders, and in this way it has gained its grasp on so many thoughtless and nervous women.

In Chicago and many other places it is said that the habit is gaining with alarming rapidity, for the women take it for every ill, and cannot believe that its soothing effect can have any evil result until the habit is thoroughly fixed upon them. It produces different results under different circumstances, and, like many other preparations, varies according to the size of the dose. In large doses it has been known to produce complete relaxation, and at the same time a loss of reflex action, and death. In moderate or tonic doses it often produces convulsions. Its effect as a stimulant seems to be very much like that of quinine, and the physicians say that they do not understand why it should get the hold on women that it does.

The latest female vice is intoxication by naphtha. It is not drank. The fumes of it are simply inhaled, inducing, so the inebriates say, a particularly agreeable exhilaration.

Remedies of Alcoholism.—Without much doubt, the best way to affect a cure is to regularly reduce one's amount of liquor each day until the system can do without it. A systematic decrease can always be carried through if the will power will back it. We add also some ideas that have been advanced by good judges: "To dispel as quickly as possible the effects of intoxicants, one of the most effectual remedies is a small dose of sal volatile, or volatile salts, in a wine-glass of water—repeating the dose in half an hour. A dish of cold broth may answer the same purpose. The most speedy way, however, of effecting a cure, is by taking an emetic, following it with the sal volatile and water half an hour after."

The Russian physician and publicist Portugaloff declares that strychnine in subcutaneous injections is an immediate and infallible remedy for drunkenness. The craving of the inebriate for drink is changed into positive aversion in a day, and after a treatment of eight or ten days the patient may be discharged. Even should the appetite return months afterward, the first attempt to resume drinking will produce such painful and nauseating sensations that the person will turn away from the liquor in disgust. The strychnine is administered by dissolving one grain in two hundred drops of water, and injecting five drops of the solution every twenty-four hours. Dr. Portugaloff recommends the establishment of inebriate dispensaries in connection with police stations.

Appetite.—Happy is the man who always possesses a good appetite; unhappy is he who does not have this precious boon. The lack of it results largely from failure of exercise and the excessive use of condiments. In the first place, try to take an invigorating bath with a wet towel and rub hard. If you cannot endure even that, use a dry towel on the body until the friction brings the blood to the surface of the skin. Then give the mouth a careful cleansing by rinsing and tooth-brush. When you sit at the table, do so with a cheerful mood, eat slowly, partake sparingly of condiments, using salt mostly, and vinegar for an acid. Preface your meals with a walk long enough to get up a circulation, if it is dinner or supper hour, but do not tire yourself, and be sure to rest the last fifteen minutes before eating.

Asphyxiation.—A practical man, conversant with cases in which asphyxiation resulted from inhaling carbonic acid gas, gives some valuable hints for their recovery by simple remedies always at hand. Fresh air to restore consciousness is the first important step. Then he gave apples, apple juice, or vinegar, to neutralize the gas and remove it from the stomach by eructations. Eggs broken into vinegar mixed and swallowed made a very effective drink. After removing the gas from the stomach, the patient was further relieved by a cup of strong, hot coffee, which speedily restored him to normal vigor. On two similar occasions, where a physician was called, he administered injections of carbonate of ammonia, and the man was ill for eight or ten days from the effects of the medicine. A little common sense is often better than physic.

Bathing.—We have already treated this subject to some extent, but we recommend the careful reading of Dr. C. H. Steele's ideas, part of which we embody here; also some other worthy opinions on this matter, of great importance to health.

"The use of water in the treatment of diseases dates back to remote antiquity. Savages resort to the surf and sweat-bath, and Hindoos and Mohammedans bathe because their religion commands them to do so. References to the bath may be found scattered throughout the literature of Greece, and in Rome the magnificent buildings and lavish expenditure devoted to the public bath show it in the highest stage of perfection it has ever attained."

"It is only within a few years past that the domestic bath has been accepted as a necessity. No home in England is complete without a bath-room, and no Englishman deems himself well unless he bathes daily. The speaker said that a thermometer, whose use should be understood, should be permanently attached to every bath-tub.

"*Physiological Action of the Bath.*—In considering the physiological action of the bath, it is first to be accepted that water of a temperature below that of the body abstracts heat from the skin, which abstraction continues indefinitely, only for a time checked by the renewed activity of the heat centers. In a bath the temperature of which is from 92° to 95°, the body may remain indefinitely without any loss or gain of temperature, but after the bath a cooling takes place, owing to increased perspirations. If the water is between 77° and 86°, there is, after the first shock, a positive rise in the temperature of the body. Sixty-five degrees, and lower, may be borne for a long time."

"Nature adapts herself to the cold bath by a rapid stimulation of heat production. All the muscles, nerves, and organs of the body are brought into heightened activity, and thus it is that to the healthy individual the cold bath is invigorating. But nature has her limits, and the bath must be discontinued while this tonic effect is felt, for the heat centers become fatigued and give rise to a chill which may continue for days afterward.

"The greatest agency in bathing is the stimulation of perspiration, and this depends upon the relative dryness of the surrounding air. Thus, in the dry vapor, or Turkish bath, a person will easily endure 264°, and lose four pounds per hour by perspiration. It is this rapid evaporation from the skin that keeps the body cool. A person may stand for some time in an oven, beside a roasting rib of beef. But in the steam or Russian bath the perspiration is retarded, and a temperature of 120° is hardly bearable. A temperature of 124° may induce a rise in the temperature of the mouth to 104° or even 107°, which is seldom reached in a raging fever. Hence, there is an element of danger in the Russian bath—a danger to sudden death similar to sunstroke. This danger is much more pronounced in the hot-water bath when perspiration ceases altogether, and the supply of heat from the interior to the skin is excessive. The temperature of bathing water should not exceed 104°, and this hot bath should not be endured more than fifteen minutes. Even then it is likely to be followed by depression and weakness." "The circulation being quickened, the cold bath acts as a good blood purifier, washing away the poisons of the body through the channels of the veins. In case of persons troubled with an excess of fat, the bath must be accompanied by massage, banting, and a liberal indulgence in outdoor exercise. In the hot bath there is this same waste of tissue, but no tonic effects, and it is invariably accompanied with loss of energy and vitality. But the action of the bath upon the skin is no less beneficial than upon the interior of the body. It favors the excretory action of the skin, thus purifying it. The millions of dead scales, kept to the skin by the clothing, and the cementing effect of the oil, are washed away, thus relieving the skin, which is the great sewerage system of the body. The work of the lungs and kidneys is thus lessened, and the danger of consumption and Bright's disease, which may be caused by uncleanness, reduced."

"*Effects of Sea Bathing.*—Sea bathing is much more tonic than all other kinds, and the reason is simple. The salt has a slightly irritating effect on the skin, which is very beneficial. Besides, sea bathing is always accompanied by the best of exercise, by relaxation and freedom from the ordinary cares of life, by a change of climate and scene. The beating of the waves against the body also has an exhilarating effect. The bath in the sea should be taken about three hours after breakfast. There are three stages experienced in the cold bath—first, that of depression; second, the tonic stage; and third, the giving out of the heat-producing powers. This is the same as the one stage of the hot bath, and is always to be avoided as highly injurious.

"Nevertheless, the hot bath has its value. Its power to cool the body is admitted, and it is used with effect in cases inflammation induced by cold.

The cold foot-bath is recommended as a positive cure for cold feet."

"The practice among modern women of taking hot baths is endangering the health of the race. In a hot bath there is at first a feeling of oppression and violent throbbing of the head, followed by prostration, a highly feverish condition, and a relaxation of the entire system. In case of any organic disease of the heart or consumption, this bath must be carefully shunned. The hot bath belongs alone to the province of the physician. The cold bath, on the other hand, aside from its tonic effects, renders the body less sensitive to changes of temperature, and in this climate is, hence, especially valuable as a protection against catching cold. This bath is from 68° to 75°, and should be taken in the morning before breakfast."

"**Bleeding.**—A sudden and profuse flow of blood is cause for alarm. First, decide whether the blood comes from an artery or a vein. If from a vein, the blood is dark, and oozes or flows evenly; if from an artery, it is bright red, and spurts in jets. In the former case, the bleeding may generally be stopped by binding on a hard pad. In case of a ruptured artery, the flow of blood may be checked by tying a twisted handkerchief, a cord, or strap, *between the wound and the heart*. If the hand is cut, raise the arm above the head and bind it tightly. In *wounds of the throat, arm-pit,* or *groin,* caused by cuts, and in case of any deep wound, thrust the thumb and finger into the bottom of the wound and pinch up the part from which the blood comes, directing the pressure against the flow. *In cuts of the lips,* compress the lips between the thumb and finger nearer the angle of the mouth than the cut itself. In *scalp wounds,* make direct pressure against the bones of the skull with the fingers, or, better, by means of a compress or bandage."

"*Nosebleed.*—Full-blooded persons who are afflicted with headache and dizziness are most subject to nosebleed. In such cases, the bleeding should be regarded as a relief to an overcharged system, and should not be too suddenly stopped. To stop the bleeding, keep the patient's arms elevated, apply cold water or ice to the base of the brain, or inject vinegar or alum water up the nostrils with a syringe. A thick piece of wrapping paper, placed between the upper lip and gum, and firmly pressed, will usually arrest the flow. It acts by compressing the arteries which supply the Sneiderian membrane. Try plugging with cotton, or a strip of soft muslin, gently pushed up the nostrils, thus causing the blood to clot about the plug. If these remedies fail, the case should have the attention of a physician."

Brain Worry.—"After a good spell of hard work, the brain worker is often tormented by finding it difficult, all at once, to turn off the steam. His workday thoughts will intrude themselves in spite of every effort to keep them out. Thackeray generally succeeded in exorcising the creatures he had been calling into existence, by the simple expedient of turning over the leaves of a dictionary. A great lawyer was in the habit, in similar circumstances, of plunging into a cold bath, and averred that a person never took out of cold water the same ideas that he took into it. Perhaps the best mental corrective of this condition is to employ the mind for a short time in a direction most contrasted to that in which it has been overworked. During excessive labor of the brain, there is an increased flow of blood to the working organ. If this condition of distention is long continued, the vessels are apt to lose the power of contracting when mental activity is diminished. Hence arises the impossibility of fulfilling the physical conditions of sleep, the most important of which is the diminution of the flow of blood to the brain. It is certain enough that the continued deprivation of any considerable part of the normal amount of sleep will be seriously detrimental to health. Dr. Hammond, in his work on sleep, mentions the case of a literary man in America who for nearly a year restricted his rest to four hours a day, and frequently less. At the end of that time, the overtasking of his mental powers was manifested in a curious way. He told the physician that, though still able to maintain a connected line of reasoning, he found that as soon as he attempted to record his ideas on paper, the composition turned out to be simply a tissue of arrant nonsense. When in the act of writing, his thoughts flowed so rapidly that he was not conscious of the disconnected nature of what he was writing, but as soon as he stopped to read it over, he was aware how completely he had misrepresented his conceptions."

Breathing.—In each respiration an adult inhales one pint of air.

A man respires 16 to 20 times a minute, or 20,000 times a day; a child, 25 to 35 times a minute.

While standing, the adult respiration is 22; while lying, 13.

The superficial surface of the lungs, *i. e.*, of their alveolar spaces, is 200 square yards. The amount of air inspired in 24 hours is about 2,500 gallons.

Two-thirds of the oxygen absorbed in 24 hours is absorbed during the night hours, from 6 P. M. to 6 A. M.

Three-fifths of the total carbonic acid is thrown off in the day-time.

The pulmonary surface gives off about 5 fluidounces of water daily in the state of vapor.

The heart sends through the lungs 192 gallons of blood hourly, or 4,608 gallons daily. The duration of inspiration is five-twelfths, of expiration seven-twelfths, of the whole respiratory act; but during sleep, inspiration occupies ten-twelfths of the respiratory period.

There are two good rules to follow given by William Blaikie:—

"1. To hold the body erect, whether standing, sitting, or walking, and breathe deeply. This habit gives the lungs and digestive organs free play. More oxygen is taken into the blood, and the food is more readily digested and assimilated. 2. To fill the lungs full at frequent intervals, holding the air in the chest as long as is comfortable. This practice will soon improve a disturbed circulation."

Bright's Disease.—Bright's disease is a disorder of the kidneys which causes those organs to secrete albumen in the urine, while they fail to extract from the blood the urea, or effete matter, which they should take up from that fluid. Urea in the blood operates as a poison, and when accumulated in large quantities, produces drowsiness, convulsions, and apoplexy. Intemperance is a fruitful source of Bright's disease, because excessive drinking tends peculiarly to the degeneration of the kidneys. The best remedy we know, or have ever seen tested, is Bethesda water, from Waukesha Springs, Wis. It should be natural, without gas; a quart per day will not be too much for an adult.

Bruises.—If the skin is not broken, the best thing for a bruise, or black and blue spot, as they are often termed, is a piece of pure copper. It should be thin enough to shape with the fingers just the curvature or angle of the portion of the body bruised. In applying it, be very gentle at first, for if it be a finger nail you desire to preserve, on first application it will give you quite a severe shock, but by relieving it every second or two, inside of 5 minutes the pain will cease, and no black spot will follow. If the skin be broken, and the blood has ceased to flow, and you desire to use this remedy, first paste a piece of unprinted newspaper over the broken part, and then proceed as above; but in no case ever place a piece of copper on a broken part of the skin without the above precaution.

Burns.—A correspondent of the Philadelphia *Record* vouches for the wonderful efficacy of the common cat-tail as a remedy for burns. He says: "Take the down, and with just enough lard to hold it together, make a plaster and lay upon any burn, and it soothes and heals so soon that it seems a miracle. Put upon a fresh burn, and in less than half an hour the smart is gone; if it is an old burn, the healing will commence in twenty-four hours. 'Cat-tail' is also the Indian remedy for scrofulous sores or ulcers. Age does not destroy its healing virtues. It can be laid away and kept for years without losing any of its remedial properties." Burns should be bathed with alcohol or turpentine and afterwards with lime-water and sweet-oil, but never with cold water. Soft soap or apple butter are equally excellent for burns.

Cancer.—It is well proved that cancer cannot be successfully removed by use of the knife. Surgeon John McFarlane, of Glasgow, mentions the cutting out of *eighty-six* cancers without effecting a *single cure*. For those who are troubled we would say that there have been and there are remedies with permanent effects. The writer knows of a female physician in this city who has been very successful in achieving lasting cures in numerous authenticated instances.

Chewing Gum and Other Substances.—Regular chewing outside of meal hours of any substance is injurious. It unnecessarily excites the salivary glands, the strength of which should be reserved for eating. Do not chew the ends of your finger nails. Little pieces of the nails may be swallowed, which at some time—possibly quite remote—may cause you great pain, and even death. This has occurred. It has also been found by opticians and doctors that hardly anything will affect the eyes harmfully quicker than gum-chewing.

Cholera.—Dr. Gamaleia, of Odessa, claims to have discovered a prophylactic against cholera, and hopes to win the prize of $20,000 offered for such a cure. He calls his specific Chemical Vaccine, and has tried it efficaciously on apes, guinea-pigs, and pigeons. This is obtained by the successive passages of cholera virus through the blood of animals. After each of these passages, the virus becomes stronger, and is finally injected into the patient.

A cure which was very effective when the cholera struck America is called the "Sun Cholera Medicine." It is also an excellent remedy for colic, and diarrhea, etc. Take equal parts of tincture of cayenne pepper, tincture of opium, tincture of rhubarb, essence of peppermint, and spirits of camphor. Mix well. Dose: 15 to 30 drops in a little cold water, according to age and violence of symptoms, repeated every fifteen minutes or twenty, until relief is obtained. Our own *infallible* remedy for cholera, cholera morbus, cramps, colic, and diarrhea, is:—

Tincture of opium, 3 drachms.
    " " cayenne pepper, 5 drachms.
    " " ginger, 5 drachms.
    " " camphor, 3 drachms.

Dose: 1 teaspoonful in a gill of cool water for an adult; repeat with half a teaspoonful in 15 minutes if not relieved. For a child 2 years old 1/4 the above dose, and in proportion up to an adult.

Cleanliness.—The English upper classes are clean, but cleanliness of any high degree is a modern virtue among them. It is an invention of the nineteenth century. Men and women born at the close of the eighteenth century did as French people do to-day; they took a warm bath occasionally for cleanliness, and they took shower-baths when they were prescribed by the physician for health, and they bathed in summer seas for pleasure, but they did not wash themselves all over every morning. However, the new custom took deep root in England, because it became one of the signs of class. It was adopted as one of the habits of a gentleman.

Don't take your pocket-handkerchief to dust off your shoes and the next moment wipe your face and eyes with it; don't carry your *own sheets* with you on a trip and then sit in the smoking-car for 200 miles for enjoyment;

anything added to white castile soap as scenting matter is no improvement and in most cases is detrimental.

We have taken this subject up so carefully in "bathing" and in the first part that we will say no more here.

Cold Feet.—The best prescription for cold or tired feet is to carefully envelop each toe and foot with blank newspaper before encasing the same with sock. First have the feet perfectly dry and warm, then they will remain so all day, if properly protected with easy-fitting, strong boots or shoes. Barbers do this to prevent their feet scalding and heating; stage drivers use this method, and hundreds attest its efficacy.

Many people, especially women and children, suffer the whole winter through with cold feet. This is mainly due to the fact that they wear their shoes too tight. Unless the toes have perfect freedom, the blood cannot circulate properly. People who wear rubbers the whole winter through, generally suffer with their feet. Rubbers make them very tender by overheating and causing them to perspire. They should be removed as soon as one enters the house. They draw the feet, keep them hot and wet with perspiration—then as soon as one goes again into the air the feet are chilled.

Colds.—Don't have any fear of night air. That is an unfounded superstition. Keep your windows open. You will sleep better and the next day you will not catch cold.

Take a good hot lemonade just before retiring; in the morning, immediately on getting out of bed, take a cold bath and rub hard until you are in a perfect glow.

Too much coddling is unquestionably one of the most common causes of catarrh. One who is inured to hardships is able to endure exposure without injury, while one unaccustomed to like experience quickly succumbs. Air-tight houses, close and unventilated, overheated rooms, even the quantity of clothing required, are active causes, preventing development of hardihood. As a result, colds and catarrh are universal maladies among civilized people.

Says a writer in *Woman's Work*: "Without dwelling on the nature and causes of colds, or on what physicians call the pathology of these disorders, I will say that a low or even starvation diet for a few days, with the free drinking of warm, mildly stimulating teas, is better for a cold than any drug or combination of drugs. If with this a warm bath or a hot foot-bath is taken, little more will be needed. Nine cases in ten of colds can be broken up in this early stage by a hot foot or rather leg-bath, keeping the bath as hot as it can be borne, until perspiration arises. After the bath drink a half pint of hot lemonade and go to bed."

A Good Cough Remedy.—The following is from a doctor connected with an institution with many children: "There is nothing more irritable to a cough than a cough. For some time I had been so fully assured of this that I determined, for one minute at least, to lessen the number of coughs heard in a certain ward in a hospital of the institution. By the promise of rewards and punishments, I succeeded in inducing them to simply hold their breath when tempted to cough, and in a little while I was myself surprised to see how some of the children entirely recovered from their disease. Constant coughing is precisely like scratching a wound on the outside of the body. So long as it is done the wound will not heal. Let a person when tempted to cough draw a long breath and hold it until it warms and soothes every air-cell, and some benefit will soon be received from this process. The nitrogen which is thus refined acts as an anodyne to the mucous membrane, allaying the desire to cough and giving the throat and lungs a chance to heal. At the same time a suitable medicine will aid nature in her effort to recuperate."

Constipation.—Regularity in the hour of going to stool and the avoidance of highly-seasoned food are preventatives. See "constipation," first part, per index, for a cure.

Consumption.—"What Changes has the Acceptance of the Germ Theory made in Measures for the Prevention and Treatment of Consumption?" is the title of an essay by Dr. Charles V. Chapin, of Providence, to whom was awarded a premium of $200 by the trustees of the Fisk Fund. In this essay Dr. Chapin has given an admirable *résumé* of all that has been written about consumption from the time of Hippocrates to the present day. After a careful examination of the literature of the subject, he thinks that we are justified in the conclusion that the acceptance of the germ theory has made no direct or important addition either to the hygiene or medicinal treatment of consumption. He thinks, however, that it should have great influence. It tells us plainly what we ought to do. We simply do not obey its behests. The germ theory—now no longer a theory in the case of tubercular consumption—tells us that we have to do with a contagious disease. Now there is no theoretical reason why a purely contagious disease like tuberculosis cannot be exterminated. If we can prevent the spread of contagion at all, we can prevent it entirely. The enormous value of preventive measures, isolation, disinfection, and quarantine, is well illustrated in history of cholera, typhus fever, and yellow fever in the United States.

By keeping out the virus of these diseases, or destroying it when it had gained access to our shores, we have for a number of years been remarkably free from these diseases, and it is certain that if these precautions had not been taken we should have suffered severely. For obvious reasons, the suppression of tuberculosis is not so easy a matter as the suppression of cholera or yellow fever. Neither is the suppression of scarlet fever or small-pox as easy. Yet whenever the public has been educated to a correct appreciation of the contagious nature of scarlet fever, the number of cases has diminished very much. Even in small-pox, with its virulent contagion, it is possible, by means of isolation and disinfection, to check its spread even among an unvaccinated population, as has been illustrated many times of late in the anti-vaccination city of Leicester, England. We must now put tuberculosis among these diseases, and, though its theoretical suppression is simple its actual extermination is a very difficult problem. It lies largely with the medical profession how long tubercular disease shall decimate the human race. The physicians are the educators of the people in these matters. When the doctor shall teach that tuberculosis is contagious, the people will believe, and will govern themselves accordingly. In combating contagious diseases the preventive measures taken often give discouraging results. This will be particularly so in tubercular disease. Half-way measures secure less than half-way results, and these alienate the support of those who only indifferently believe in contagion and the importance of precautionary measures. Efficient means of suppression are radical, and bear hard on the individual; they are not complied with, and they produce violent opposition. Yet, difficult as it may be, the medical profession should take aggressive action against this disease. We have no right to wait for the discovery of a specific, or the gradual evolution of a phthisis-proof race. We must take the world as we find it, full of men and women predisposed to tubercular phthisis, and with no idea of its contagious nature. What can we do about it? 1. Teach the people the true nature of the tuberculosis, that no one ever has tubercular consumption unless the tubercle bacilli find their way into their lungs. 2. Teach them, also, that, even if it finds its way there, it will not grow unless the conditions are right. Teach fathers and mothers how to rear healthy boys and girls. Tell them what to eat and what to wear, to exercise, to breathe fresh air. This alone would exterminate phthisis. 3. The contagion must be destroyed. Fortunately, in this disease there is no need of isolation. Disinfection is enough. The consumptive patient gives off the poison only in the sputum, or perchance the other excreta, if the disease extend beyond the lungs. The virus is not given off from these while moist. We must therefore disinfect all sputum at once with mercuric bi-chloride. Cloths must be used instead of handkerchiefs, and then burned, or, if the latter are used, they should be often changed, and immediately put in a bi-chloride solution and boiled. Bed-linen should be treated in the same way. Frequent disinfection of the entire person, and fumigation of the apartment, would be safe additions to the preventive measures. 4. Persons who have a marked predisposition to the disease had best not come in close contact with the phthisical. Children should never have tuberculous nurses, wet or dry. In the case of consumptives very great attention should be paid to ventilation, and to the alimentation both of the patient and the attendants. Such measures, if rigidly carried out, would be of enormous service in preventing this disease. But with the increasing prevalence of tuberculosis among domestic animals, something more is imperatively demanded. Active measures should be taken to free the country from animal tuberculosis.

There are some ideas which it is well to observe:—

1. Flies may carry the virus if they are allowed to frequent cuspidors into which consumptives have expectorated. Clean these out often. Do not permit the patient to spit into a handkerchief and then let it lie around to dry. The dust arising may inoculate some person prone to consumption.

2. Be careful about the meat you eat. It can and does convey tuberculosis. Investigations have been made showing that as high as 50% of a herd to be slaughtered in New York City had tuberculosis. Milk may be also infected and often is.

3. Have an abundance of flowers around. They invariably are helpful.

4. Constant and regular singing with proper care and not tiring is excellent for consumptive lungs, which should be done in well-ventilated rooms.

5. Be out in the open air as much as possible, and breathe through the nose entirely. Continually exercise the lungs by drawing in long breaths.

6. If possible try fumes of hydrofluoric acid. In glass factories if workmen are rendered consumptive by stooping over the grinding machinery, they usually find great benefit by being allowed to work in the room with the glass etchers, where so much hydrofluoric acid is employed.

7. Buttermilk is well recommended.

8. Consumptive and bronchial troubles in women are often due to irregularity of dress about the throat and lungs. There is danger from wearing *décolléte* costumes. So regular have we been in our habits that the throwing off of a 1-oz. neck-tie for half an hour in the open air will give us a cold with the thermometer at 70% Fahr.

The ocean cure is well set forth in the following, which represents the advantages of a long sea voyage:—

1. Perfect rest and quiet, and complete removal from and change of ordinary occupation and way of life; a very thorough change of scene, and perfect and enforced rest from both mental and physical labor.

2. The life in the open air and the great amount of sunshine to be enjoyed; it is quite possible, under favorable circumstances, to pass fifteen hours daily in the open air; and whenever it is possible the traveler by sea is certain to endeavor to escape from the close and sometimes unpleasant atmosphere of a small cabin, into the pure air to be found on deck.

3. The great purity of the air at sea, and its entire freedom from organic dust and other impurities. In this respect it has an advantage over the air of an open country, for the latter is apt to contain the pollen of grasses and other plants, which, in some persons, excites hay fever and asthma. The air of the cabins may, of course, be contaminated, but the air of the open sea is probably the purest to be found anywhere.

4. The presence in the sea air of a large amount of ozone, as well as particles of saline matter, more particularly in stormy weather, from the sea spray, and these may exercise a beneficial effect in certain throat and pulmonary affections on the respiratory mucous membrane.

5. The great equability of the temperature at sea. This refers chiefly to the daily variations, which rarely exceed four or five degrees Fahr. It must be noted that in a long sea voyage very considerable variations of temperature are encountered, and in a swift steamer the transitions are somewhat sudden.

6. The great humidity of the atmosphere and the high barometric pressure, which are considered to exercise a useful sedative influence on certain constitutions. It is said that the temperature of the body averages one degree Fahr. less on account of this sedative effect. The exhilarating and tonic effect of rapid motion through the air; for by the continuous progress of the ship the sea breezes are constantly blowing over it, and the passengers are borne through the rapidly-moving air without any exertion of their own. The influence of these currents of air on the surface of the body is, no doubt, important, acting as a stimulant and a tonic, increasing evaporation from the skin, and imparting tone to the superficial blood-vessels.

We now give our own cure, which we claim is of great value, at least it is worth trying, for it cured the author of consumption of twenty years' standing in one year. This disease can be cured by "cold packing" the lungs and throat, and following the rules in general for health stated in the first part of this work. You must understand a cold compress or pack, otherwise you are likely to increase the malady and hasten your death. Some persons cannot warm one ounce of cold water in twenty-four hours. Such we advise to go very slowly. First adopt the formulæ for cleanliness and regularity already given. Then when a little more blood is infused through the system and hence more heat exists, commence the cold pack. Use simply a moistened cambric handkerchief, placed upon the lungs; envelop with at least two thicknesses of linen and one of flannel; wrap up warm and go to bed. Do not attempt to cold pack any part of your body and then expose it to a moving atmosphere. After one week you can increase the moisture of the pack at least 50%. Then add to the thickness and moisture 10% each week, as long as you can succeed in warming it and causing it to sweat that portion of the body packed. If you should wake up in the night and find the pack dry, remove the portion previously moistened and retain only the dry covering, viz., the linen and flannel. In the morning, before arising, thoroughly rub the lungs with a dry linen towel. This, then, is all that is necessary to get rid of this incurable (?) disease, if you will only follow the rules already given for health, happiness, and longevity.

Convulsions, Fits.—When a child has a convulsion, or what is commonly called "a fit," attention should be given to the urinary secretion at once. If there is suppression of urine, the child should be put into a warm bath and made to sweat as speedily as possible. In many cases in which children die from a succession of convulsions, the real cause of death is suppression of urine (a fact which is probably not so generally known as it should be), so that the child really dies of poisoning through the retention of the urinary secretion. When a child is subject to attacks of this character, care should be taken to dress it warmly in flannels, so as to keep up a degree of perspiration most of the time, and hot baths should be administered frequently. Give a glass of Bethesda water from three to four times a day, and the disease will disappear.

Corns and Bunions are caused by tight, ill-fitting boots and shoes. The way of preventing them is, therefore, manifest. Thrusting the toe into a lemon, to be kept on over night, will make the removal of a corn easy. Two or three applications will suffice for the worst cases. Soft corns may be relieved by dissolving a piece of ammonia, the size of three peas, in an ounce of water, and applying the solution as hot as can be borne. It is beneficial to place blank newspaper between the toes. That will keep them from scalding, and hence softening, so that corns will easily form. We have already referred to this paper method for cold feet. Paper is a non-conductor and thus has the proper effect.

Croup.—The following prescription, to be used as a gargle, is not only excellent for croup, but will *absolutely* keep anyone from choking to death from phlegm in the throat, no matter what the cause, so long as they have any portion of a lung left. It consists of the yolks of two eggs thoroughly beaten, in half a pint of good cider vinegar, adding two tablespoonfuls of honey. I have known two different patients, given up by their physicians, to rally in thirty minutes under the above treatment, and finally get well.

Diabetes.—A prominent French physician advocates a coffee remedy. After having continued to use the remedy for upward of a third of a century in many hundreds of cases, he again appeals to the profession to give it a trial in those cases of liver and kidney troubles which have resisted all other treatment. His habit is to place twenty-five grammes, or about three drachms, of the green berries (he prefers a mixture of three parts of Mocha with one part each of Martinique and Isle de Bourbon coffee) in a tumbler of cold water, and let them infuse over night. The infusion, after straining or filtering, is to be taken on an empty stomach the first thing after getting up in the morning. He cites many cases of renal and hepatic colics, diabetes, migraine, etc., which, although rebellious to all other treatments for years, soon yielded to the green coffee infusion. It is worth a trial at any rate.

Bethesda water from the Wakeshaw Springs, in Wisconsin, will cure three out of every five cases of diabetes and help the other two. Drink it as you would any good water.

Diphtheria.—Diphtheria is a malignant and very infectious disease. It may often be communicated by a kiss, a touch of the hand, or by drinking out of the same cup with the sick person. The mildest case should be carefully isolated. In the family this may sometimes be done by removing the patient to an upper room, which can be well ventilated by means of windows and an open fire. The contagion of diphtheria is not carried far by the atmosphere; hence, by strict attention to cleanliness and ventilation, it may be quite possible to isolate a case even under the family roof. The disease is characterized by soreness of the throat, pain in swallowing, apoplectic, epileptic, hysterical, or the result of poisoning. Put a cork between the patient's teeth, that the tongue may not be bitten. Loosen the clothing, have plenty of fresh air, and do not restrain the movements of the patient, except to prevent injury or bruising. Rub the temples with cologne or spirits, and, as soon as the patient can swallow, give a little cold brandy and water.

Dr. W. A. Scott, of Iowa, where, in the latter part of 1889, diphtheria raged, found a valuable and effective remedy for this dread disease. The recipe can be filled at any drug store, and used by any person without danger:—

Take ten grains of permanganate of potassium and mix with one ounce of cold water. As soon as dissolved, it must be applied with a rag or sponge mop or swab to the whitish places in the tonsils, and other parts that have the diphtheria membrane on them. Do this very gently, but thoroughly, every three hours until better; then every six hours until well. It does not give pain, but is rather nauseous to the taste.

If the tongue is coated white, mix one drachm of hyposulphite of soda and five drops oil of sassafras in four ounces of syrup made of sugar and hot water, and give a teaspoonful every 1 to 3 hours, as needed, when awake.

If the tongue is not coated white, I mix 20 drops of tincture of phytolacca in four ounces of cold water and give a teaspoonful every 1 to 3 hours, as needed, when awake. (The phytolacca is the common poke-root of the South, and as it loses its strength by drying and age, the tincture should be from the fresh root, or it is worthless.)

It is well to apply a little sweet-oil or cosmoline to the outside of the throat to protect from the action of the air, as the patient must be protected from all danger of getting chilled.

In the beginning of the disease, in mild cases, the above solution of permanganate of potassium is all I use, and all that is needed, as the disease is local at first, but rapidly affects the whole system when seated. In the stinking form of diphtheria this solution soon destroys all smell, and in every case destroys the diphtheria membrane without leaving any bad effect.

M. Roulin, of France, has successfully treated 22 cases of diphtheria with carbolic acid as an antiseptic. Nasal douches, consisting of three teaspoonfuls of the crude acid in a quart of water, were employed every hour by means of the ordinary irrigator. Tonics were given internally.

Dr. Deriker, of St. Petersburg, who is the head physician of the Children's Hospital, and has treated no less than 2,000 cases of diphtheria, and tried all remedies, both internal and external, has found the following a certain cure for the disease: As soon as the white spots appear on the tonsils he gives a laxative, usually senna tea. When the purgative effect has ceased, he gives cold drinks acidulated with lemons, limes, or hydrochloric acid, and every two hours a gargle composed of lime-water and milk. Hot milk was also given as a drink, and the throat well rubbed with spirits of turpentine. The

Academy of Medicine in France offered a large sum of money for a successful cure for diphtheria, and this is said to have been it. Equal parts of liquid tar and turpentine are put in an iron pan and burned in the patient's room. The dense resinous smoke gives immediate relief. The fibrinous matter soon becomes detached and is coughed up.

Clothing.—There are some very important principles in regard to dress:—

1. If you desire health, do not wear a belt.

2. Avoid tight lacing. Some of the most beautiful women, including actresses, are giving up this injurious practice.

3. Do not wear, especially in summer, the constant black, even if in mourning. If you do someone may be mourning you too.

4. Use woolens almost entirely for clothing—always for under-clothing.

5. Have shoes that fit and give the feet an abundance of room, and not high heeled, but thick soled.

6. Wear sufficiently heavy woolen under-garments so that you will not be obliged to resort continually to overcoats.

7. In summer, use light outer garments—white flannels and cheviots are excellent.

THE MOST IMPORTANT FUNCTION OF UNDER-GARMENTS.—It is a great mistake to suppose that the material of which a garment is made is the most important consideration in selecting warm under-clothing. The way in which the fabric is prepared and manufactured is of more vital importance as regards heat or coldness of the body than the actual material. A light garment with large meshes is more effective against cold than a close, heavy one. Whatever an under-vest may be made of, its real value as a protector from cold depends upon its ability to inclose within its meshes a certain quantity of air. This is indeed the most important function of under-garments, viz., to encircle the whole body with an envelope of warm air, and a vestment that does not keep a continual layer of warm air next to the skin is of very little use.

We advise the discarding of cotton shirts altogether and wearing only those of flannel. The best material for an under-vest, where the shirt worn is flannel, is silk, but by reason of high cost it is within the reach of a comparatively few only.

Hence woolen under-vests must be selected. They should be large and never tight-fitting, for there must be room for the air to circulate freely beneath them. Good taste suggests that the outside shirt be of white flannel, and that also must be large. Nearly all those which are on sale in stores have collars, but for a small sum added to the price the dealer will make the necessary changes so that a linen collar may be worn.

With such under-clothing a man is very well protected against sudden changes of weather, and is much less liable to take cold than he would be with a cotton shirt on. Now, as to chest protectors. If a man is subject to colds during the winter he should wear a chest-protector. In order for him to get the full benefit of it it should fit him quite snugly at the neck and extend front and back to the belt. Dressed in flannels, as we have recommended, with his chest well covered by a protector, he will be as well fortified against cold as under-clothing of a healthful sort can make him.

Dropsy.—It is not generally known that the silk on an ear of green corn is a powerful and efficient remedy for dropsy, for bladder troubles and diseases of the kidneys. In the Louisville *Medical News* we find an account of the medical properties of corn-silk and the cures that have been effected by its use. The way to use it is to take two double-handfuls of fresh corn-silk and boil in two gallons of water until but a gallon remains. Add sugar to make a syrup. Drink a tumblerful of this thrice daily, and it will relieve dropsy by increasing the flow of urine. Other diseases of the bladder and kidneys are benefited by the remedy, which is prompt, efficient, and grateful to the stomach. The treatment can be continued for months without danger or inconvenience. Bethesda water is just as good, but both together are better.

Dyspepsia.—This trouble is often the result of decomposition of the food before it is digested. Unless this is remedied death will ultimately follow. A good remedy is this: Thoroughly brown some whole grain wheat, grind it in an ordinary clean coffee-mill; eat of nothing else for the two last meals of the day; carefully masticate it and eat sparingly for a few days, after that *ad* *libitum*; in ten days you will be well, if all other suggestions regarding cleanliness are followed.

Ears.—Sapolini of Milan has described a method of his which he states has been successfully employed in 62 cases of deafness of old age. It consists in mopping the membrana tympani with a weak oleaginous solution of phosphorus. He claims that the treatment diminishes the opacity of the membrane, increases the circulation, and improves the hearing.

A writer in a medical journal says: "Beware of too much quinine. It will produce a congestion of the ear and irritation of the auditory nerve. The common habit of taking quinine for neuralgia and other ailments without consulting a doctor is altogether reprehensible, and may lead to very serious results. Many cases of deafness are produced by overdoses and long-continued use of this drug."

Aprysexie is the name Dr. Guye, of Amsterdam, chooses for inattentiveness, and he quite singularly finds that the nose is a cause of it. A dull boy became quick to learn after certain tumors had been taken from the nose, and a man who had been troubled with vertigo and buzzing in the ears for twelve years found mental labor easy after a like operation. In a third case a medical student was similarly relieved. Dr. Guye supposes that these nasal troubles affect the brain by preventing the cerebral lymph from circulating freely.

Elixir Brown-Sequard.—The way Brown-Sequard uses this medicine is entirely successful. Do not think because others have failed that the principle is wrong. Most experimenters, first, are not careful in getting perfectly healthy specimens of animals from whose vitals the elixir is made, while, secondly, they expose the liquid and allow it to become filled or impregnated with microbes and various foreign elements.

The process of administration is thus described:—

The syringe punctures the cuticle, or scarf-skin, and the cutis, or true skin, and then enters the subcutaneous or cellular tissue which covers the muscles, or flesh. Through all the tissues of the body run the lymphatics, which convey the injected matter to the lymph channels, these in turn to the veins, and thence throughout the system. A half ounce of the fluid will be distributed in from one to three hours. Sometimes the subject might feel the stimulus very quickly, and in some cases hours might elapse before any effect was felt. The human system is able to absorb almost an unlimited amount of this liquid, if administered properly and if pure.

Epidemics.—The history of severe plagues is remarkable. The first great pestilence in a comparatively civilized nation was the one at Athens about 400 B. C. On account of being shut up by the Spartans in their crowded city the Athenians had this terrible experience. It carried off thousands—nearly two-thirds of the population. In the reign of the Emperor Justinian no less than 100,000,000 inhabitants died in thirty years from a pestilence that swept from Persia to Gaul. Later, in the fourteenth century, the plague of beautiful Florence in Italy killed 80,000 people in six months. In 1665-66 London was a vast pest-house and during September of 1666 the weekly death rate reached the number of 8,000. In America the sunny South has witnessed the blasting effects of yellow fever during the last fifteen years. In 1878, Florida had 2,649 deaths, and New Orleans 3,977 from yellow fever. Fully 33% of those attacked succumbed. In the same year 4,200 people died of it at Memphis. The last important run of this epidemic was in 1888, at Jacksonville and Decatur. There the deaths averaged 10% of those attacked.

The duration of the infection stages of various diseases is thus given by Dr. T. F. Pearse, an English physician: Measles, from the 2d day of the disease for 3 weeks; small-pox, from the 1st day for 4 weeks; scarlet fever, from the 4th day for 7 weeks; mumps, from the 2d day for 3 weeks; diphtheria, from the 1st day for 3 weeks. The incubation periods, or intervals occurring between exposure to infection and the first symptoms, are as follows: Whooping-cough, 14 days; mumps, 18 days; measles, 10 days; small-pox, 12 days; scarlet fever, 3 days; diphtheria, 14 days.

Scarlet fever is at its minimum from January to May, and at its maximum in October and November. Diphtheria is more evenly distributed through the year, and is most dangerous a little later than scarlet fever. Measles and whooping-cough seem to be somewhat aggravated by cold weather, but are most fatal in May and June. Hot weather is adverse to small-pox, and favorable to disorders of the bowels, particularly in children.

THE DIFFERENCE BETWEEN MEASLES AND SMALL-POX.—At the outset of a popular eruption it is often difficult to decide whether the case is one of measles or of small-pox. M. Grisol's method of diagnosis is as follows (*Medical Times*): "If, upon stretching a portion of the skin, the papule becomes impalpable to the touch, the eruption is caused by measles; if, on the contrary, the papule is still felt when the skin is drawn out, the eruption is the result of small-pox."

Erysipelas.—It has long been known that an attack of erysipelas exerts a remarkable influence upon other diseases, and the attempt has been made to cure more serious maladies by deliberately inoculating the patient with the virus of erysipelas. In a recent case in Norway, the growth of a cancer was greatly retarded by this means, and life was probably prolonged a few weeks or even months, though no cure was effected.

Exercise.—Ben. Hogan, the reformed pugilist, has advanced some practical ideas:—

"In every city there are thousands of rich men and women who are ready to commit suicide because of ill-health. 'What is wealth without health?' they say. 'Nothing,' I should say; but I do say that, while every man cannot amass wealth, every man can secure good health. I know a man who owns a fine horse. He employs two men to take care of that horse and keep him in condition. He is exercised, sponged, and blanketed daily. Does the owner himself have a man to take care of him?—No. He possibly bathes once a week. He arises at 8 o'clock in the morning, throws his breakfast down without masticating it, and madly rushes off to his business. At noon he rushes into a restaurant and eats his dinner in five minutes. On he goes, hiring men to look after the health of his horse, but never stops to think of his own body and its needs.

"A man cannot digest his food unless he eats carefully. A meal should never be eaten in less than one hour. Gladstone says he bites each piece of meat he puts into his mouth twenty times before he swallows it, and that isn't too often. The men of to-day who throw their food into their stomach are physical wrecks in fifteen years. The American doctor studies medicine when he should study nature; instead of trying to prevent disease, they try to cure. There are many people who do not take a bath in two years and they prematurely die from poisoning. The poison that accumulates under the first layer of skin breeds disease and sooner or later must come death.

"There are thousands of people dying of consumption who haven't sense enough to know that they can throw it off. No man who is lazy can become healthy, for the best way to bring health is by physical development. I have seen thousands of young men apparently on the verge of the grave grow strong by following this daily routine: When you get up in the morning rub yourself with a rough towel until the blood is in circulation, and then take a cold bath. Never take a cold bath without getting the blood in circulation, for it is dangerous. After the bath rub the flesh for three-quarters of an hour. Then take a cup of tea and eat some toast, and start out for a half hour's walk. Don't plod slowly along the streets, but walk as rapidly as your legs will carry you. When you return you are ready for breakfast. Eat rice, mutton chops, and toast, and drink tea. If you are a business man you are ready for business, but if you are training for an athlete you will again start upon the walk and keep it up all day. A man under training is required to walk at least forty miles every day. When he returns from his walk he is put under blankets until he has cooled, and then again put in the bath-tub. He is taken out and rubbed or manipulated. Then he is ready for dinner. The athlete or pugilist would be required to eat raw ham or raw steak without salt or pepper. Pugilists are not allowed to use pepper, because it heats the blood. For men who are not undergoing training for pugilists I would advise a dinner on rare beef, rice, and other vegetables cooked dry."

Eyes.—A writer in *Cassell's Magazine* gives the following rules for the use and care of the eyes:—

"1. Sit erect in your chair when reading, and as erect when writing as possible. If you bend downward you not only gorge the eyes with blood, but the brain as well, and both suffer. The same rule should apply to the use of the microscope. Get one that will enable you to look at things horizontally, not always vertically.

"2. Have a reading-lamp for night use. N. B.—In reading the light should be on the book or paper and the eyes in the shade. If you have no reading-lamp, turn your back to the light and you may read without danger to your eyes.

"3. Hold the book at your focus; if that begins to get far away use spectacles.

"4. Avoid reading by the flickering light of the fire.

"5. Avoid straining the eyes by reading in the gloaming.

"6. Reading in bed is injurious as a rule. It must be admitted, however, that in cases of sleeplessness, when the mind is inclined to ramble over a thousand thoughts a minute, reading steadies the thoughts and conduces to sleep.

"7. Do not read much in a railway carriage. I myself always do, however, only in a good light, and I invariably carry a good reading-lamp to hang on behind me. Thousands of people would travel by night rather than by day if the companies could only see their way to the exclusive use of the electric light.

"8. Authors should have black-ruled paper instead of blue, and should never strain the eyes by reading too fine types.

"9. The bedroom blinds should be red or gray, and the head of the bed should be toward the window.

"10. Those ladies who not only write but sew should not attempt the black seam by night.

"11. When you come to an age that suggests the wearing of spectacles, let no false modesty prevent you from getting a pair. If you have only one eye, an eye-glass will do; otherwise it is folly.

"12. Go to the wisest and best optician you know of and state your wants and your case plainly, and be assured you will be properly fitted.

"13. Remember that bad spectacles are most injurious to the eyes, and that good and well-chosen ones are a decided luxury.

"14. Get a pair for reading with, and if necessary a long-distance pair for use outdoors."

Further rules are:—

Avoid all sudden changes between light and darkness.

Never begin to read, write, or sew for several minutes after coming from darkness to a bright light.

Never read by twilight or moonlight, or on dark, cloudy days.

When reading, it is best to let the light fall from above obliquely over the left shoulder.

Do not use the eye-sight by light so scant that it requires an effort to discriminate.

The moment you are instinctively prompted to rub your eyes that moment stop using them.

If the eyelids are glued together on waking up do not forcibly open them, but apply saliva with the finger. It is the speediest diluent in the world; then wash your eyes and face in warm water.

In the selection of books or pamphlets see that the paper is of a slight orange tint; this shade is the most pleasant for the eye to look upon.

The following is recommended as an efficient means of removing particles from the eye: Make a loop by doubling a horse hair; raise the lid of the eye in which is the foreign particle; slip the loop over it, and placing the lid in contact with the eyeball, withdraw the loop, and the particle will be drawn out with it.

An old locomotive engineer gives the following as an infallible method to eradicate any foreign substance from the eye, viz., close the eyes, and rub gently from right to left with a circular motion the well eye.

Food.—Of all the fruits we are blest with, the peach is the most digestible. There is nothing more palatable, wholesome, and medicinal than good, ripe peaches. They should be ripe but not overripe and half rotten; and of this kind they may make a part of either meal, or be eaten between meals; but it is better to make them a part of the regular meals, says *Hall's Journal of Health*, a medical authority. It is a mistaken idea that no fruit should be eaten at breakfast. It would be far better if our people would eat less bacon and grease at breakfast and more fruit. In the morning there is an arid state of the secretions, and nothing is so well calculated to correct this as cooling, subacid fruits, such as peaches, apples, etc. The apple is one of the best of fruits. Baked or stewed apples will generally agree with the most delicate stomach, and are an excellent medicine in many cases of sickness. Green or half-ripe apples stewed and sweetened are pleasant to the taste, cooling, nourishing, and laxative, far superior, in many cases, to the abominable doses of salts and oil usually given in fever and other diseases. Raw apples and dried apples stewed are better for constipation than liver pills. Oranges are very acceptable to most stomachs, having all the advantages of the acid alluded to; but the orange juice alone should be taken, rejecting the pulp. The same may be said of lemonade, pomegranates, and all that class. Lemonade is the best drink in fevers, and when thickened with sugar is better than syrup of squills and other nauseants in many cases of cough. Tomatoes act on the liver and bowels, and are much more pleasant and safe than blue mass and "liver regulators." The juice should be used alone, rejecting the skins. The small-seeded fruits, such as blackberries, figs, raspberries, currants, and strawberries, may be classed among the best foods and medicines. The sugar in them is nutritious, the acid is cooling and purifying, and the seeds are laxative. We would be much the gainers if we would look more to our orchards and gardens for our medicines and less to our drug stores. To cure fever or act on the kidneys no febrifuge or diuretic is superior to water-melon, which may, with very few exceptions, be taken in sickness and health in almost unlimited quantities, not only without injury but with positive benefit. But in using them the water or juice should be taken, excluding the pulp, and the melon should be ripe and fresh, but not overripe and stale. While, undeniably, a mixed diet is the best for man, there is a mistaken notion, which prevails to a great extent, that meat should largely enter into the same. As a consequence, much more is eaten than is needed or can properly be disposed of in the system. Never eat meat oftener than once a day, and very sparingly in summer. Men of sedentary habits might with safety for several days at a time during that season live on vegetables, fruits, milk, breadstuffs, and foods of like character, which are easy of digestion. For those who have good reason to believe that their "kidneys are weak," a diet largely made up of meat is ill-advised. Those organs are intimately concerned in its disposal in the system, and hence are overtasked if it is taken in too great a quantity.

Reasons Why a Strictly Vegetable Diet Is to Be Preferred to Animal Food.—
The food which is most enjoyed, says a writer in *Longman's Magazine*, is the food we call bread and fruit. In my long medical career, I have rarely known an instance in which a child has not preferred fruit to animal food. I have been many times called upon to treat children for stomachic disorders induced by pressing upon them animal to the exclusion of fruit diet, and have seen the best results occur from the practice of reverting to the use of fruit in the dietary. I say it without the least prejudice, as a lesson learned from simple experience, that the most natural diet for the young, after the natural milk diet, is fruit and whole-meal bread, with milk and water for drink. The desire for this same mode of sustenance is often continued into after years, as if the resort to flesh were a forced and artificial feeding, which required long and persistent habit to establish as a permanency as a part of the system of every-day life. How strongly this preference taste for fruit over animal food prevails is shown by the simple fact of the retention of those foods in the mouth. Fruit is retained, to be tasted and relished. Animal food, to use a common phrase, is "bolted." There is a natural desire to retain the delicious fruit for full mastication; there is no such desire, except in the trained gormand, for the retention of animal substance. One further fact which I have observed—and that too often to discard it—as a fact of great moment, is that when a person of mature years has for a time given up voluntarily the use of animal food in favor of vegetable, the sense of repugnance to animal food is soon so markedly developed that a return to it is overcome with the utmost difficulty. Neither is this a mere fancy or fad peculiar to sensitive men or oversentimental women. I have been surprised to see it manifested in men who are the very reverse of sentimental, and who were, in fact, quite ashamed to admit themselves guilty of any such weakness. I have heard those who have gone over from a mixed diet of animal and vegetable food to a poor vegetable diet speak of feeling low under the new system, and declare that they must needs give it up in consequence; but I have found even these (without exception) declare that they infinitely preferred the simpler, purer, and, as it seemed to them, more natural food plucked from the prime source of food, untainted by its passage through another animal body.

There are thirty vegetarian restaurants in London, and a vegetarian hotel is the latest move in the right direction.

The time required to digest different kinds of food:—

	Hours
Roasted pork	5.15
Salt beef (boil'd)	4.15
Veal (boiled)	4.00
Boiled hens	4.00
Roasted mutton	3.15
Boiled beef	3.30
Roasted beef	3.00
Raw oysters	2.45
Roasted turkey	2.30
Boiled milk	2.00
Boiled codfish	2.00
Venison steak	1.35
Trout (broiled)	1.30
Tripe	1.00
Pig's feet	1.00
Eggs (hard boil'd)	3.30 to 5.30
Eggs (soft boil'd)	3.00

The above is taken from Beaumont's "Experiments on Digestion." Dalton comments on these observations as follows: "These results would not always be precisely the same for different persons, since there are variations in this respect according to age and temperament. Thus, in most instances, mutton would probably be equally digestible with beef, or perhaps more so; and milk, which in some persons is easily digested, in others is disposed of with considerable difficulty. But as a general rule, the comparative digestibility of different substances is no doubt correctly expressed by the above list."

To Ascertain Pure Milk.—Take an extra quart of milk any day from your milkman and put it in a glass jar, an ordinary fruit-jar will do; set it away and await results. The proportion of cream on top shows the richness of the milk. Let it alone until it turns to clabber, and if there is any water in it, it will appear between the cream and the clabber. After fermentation sets in, the water will sink to the bottom. If there has been no water put into the milk, none will show. By trying milk from different milkmen, you can readily see which is the best.

We will add under food that eggs should be kept in oak or porcelain receptacles, not in pine boxes, as they partake of the odor of the pine.

Freckles.—A young lady of St. Louis says: "I accidentally discovered a sovereign remedy a couple of years ago, which costs next to nothing. One day the plumber shut our water off, and I could get none in which to wash my face. I was fearfully soiled, and, looking out of the window just then, I saw a friend approaching to call on me. Glancing about me, I noticed half a water-melon from which the meat had been removed some time before. It was partly filled with juice, and I hastily washed my face in it. The result was so soothing that I repeatedly washed my face in that manner. Judge of my astonishment a few days later on seeing that there was not a freckle left on my face."

Gargle.—An excellent gargle for general use is:—

Chloras Potass., 3 ounces.
Tannin, 2 drachms.

Dissolve one teaspoonful in half a pint of water, which will keep for several days. For bronchial trouble or bleeding at the lungs, gargle the throat often; but for general cleanliness, gargle a little every morning; for catarrh, not only gargle but snuff some up the nose.

Hair.—To prevent hair from falling out, headache, neuralgia, brain fever, etc., the hair should be worn comparatively short by both sexes, washed and dried every day. To preserve the hair this is a good recipe: Take a teaspoonful of dried sage; boil it in a quart of water for twenty minutes. Strain it off and add a piece of borax the size of an English walnut; pulverize the borax. Put the sage tea, when cold, into a quart bottle; add the borax; shake well together and put in a cool place. Brush the hair thoroughly and rub and wash well on the head with the hand; then, after a good hard rubbing, brush the hair well before a fire, so that it will become perfectly dry. Never use a fine-tooth comb, as it irritates the skin, and consequently inflames the roots of the hair.

Headache.—The causes are: "Overstudy, overwork in-doors, neglect of the bath, want of fresh air in bedrooms, nervousness, however induced; want of abundant skin-exciting exercise, the excitement inseparable from a fashionable life, neglect of the ordinary rules that conduce to health, overindulgence in food, especially of a stimulating character, weakness or debility of body, however produced (this can only be remedied by proper nutriment), work or study in-doors, carried on in an unnatural or cramped position of the body. Literary men and women ought to do most of their work at a standing desk, lying down now and then to ease the brain and heart, and permit ideas to flow. They should work out-of-doors in fine weather—with their feet resting on a board, not on the earth—and under canvas in wet weather. It is surprising the good this simple advice, if followed, can effect.

Health Beverages.—Lemons make the best beverage. They are very healthy and good, not only for allaying the thirst, but will cure a multitude of disorders. The juice of the lemon contains citric acid. Acids, as a rule, decrease the acid secretion of the body and increase the alkaline. Citric acid, which is the acid of lemons and oranges, for instance, will diminish the secretions of gastric juice, but increases very materially the secretion of saliva. The very thought of a lemon is sufficient to make the mouth water. Thirst in fevers is not always due to lack of water in the blood. It may be due in part to a lack of the secretion of the saliva. When the mouth is parched and dry, the acid will increase the saliva. When acid is given for the relief of dyspepsia it should be taken before eating. Lemon juice drank before meals will be found very advantageous as a preventive of heart-burn.

Drinks for the Voice.—Tea, coffee, and cocoa are three admissible drinks, but none in excess. For the voice cocoa is the most beneficial. It should never be made too strong, and those cocoas are the best that have been deprived of their oil. A cup of thin cocoa, just warm, is more to be recommended between the exertions of singing than any alcoholic beverage. Tea must not be taken too strong, nor when it has drawn too long, for tea then becomes acid, and has a bad influence on the mucous membrane that lines the throat. There is always a dry sensation after having taken a cup of tea that has been allowed to draw too long. A vocalist had better do without sugar in tea and only take milk with it.

Hernia or Rupture.—A swelling suddenly appearing in the abdomen, and especially in the groin, may be recognized as a rupture, particularly if it puffs out, or grows larger when the patient breathes or coughs violently. If, for any reason, the services of a physician cannot be immediately secured, the patient should lie down on his back, draw up his knees, and, while he breathes gently, rest his fingers upon the rupture, and press it in all directions. In most cases the hernia will slip back when thus treated. Then apply a bandage to hold the bowels in place long enough for the person to have a truss fitted to him. During this period the bowels should be kept regular.

The author of this book was cured of rupture of the right groin completely. Though having worn trusses of different patterns for 25 years, the one that effected a permanent remedy was an electric elastic truss, invented by Dr. A. T. Sherwood, 408 Stockton Street, this city. This is no advertisement, but wishing to help others who are afflicted, we are of the opinion that it will cure four out of every five cases that exist, provided the patient will pursue a careful course otherwise. My treatment required less than 4 months.

Hiccoughing.—Sweet-flag (calamus) is claimed to be an agent that will relieve and stop persistent hiccough in almost any case. Chew a small piece of the root.

Hydrophobia.—Rabies, the madness produced by the bite of mad animals, is often apprehended when there is no danger. In case the supposed mad creature has been killed, an important means of information is lost. If possible, the animal should be secured and closely watched. If he does not show signs of rabies, the bitten person need have no fear; but, in any case, when one has been bitten, the wound should be washed with hot water, sucked, by some person whose mouth is free from sores, and then thoroughly cauterized with pure nitric acid or concentrated liquor of ammonia. The patient's strength should be sustained by stimulants, and medical attendance should be secured as soon as possible.

Drs. Valentine Mott and A. F. Baldwin, of the Carnegie Laboratory; are prepared to inoculate hydrophobia patients according to the Pasteur system.

The first patient was the seven-year-old son of Dr. Newell, of Jersey City. Dr. Mott inoculated himself to prove the harmlessness of the method for a healthy man.

It has been discovered recently that the juice of the maguey plant is a certain remedy for hydrophobia.

Influenza (La Grippe).—The first symptoms of the disease are sudden faintness, a chill, and marked prostration, succeeded by headache and a general feeling of malaria, followed by acute coryza, pharyngitis, and slight laryngitis, winding up with bronchitis. Examination shows that the patients are about as sick as persons with a bad cold. The duration of the attack is from 2 to 10 days and upward. An application of 2 parts turpentine to 1 of sweet-oil placed on the chest over the lungs, and then inhale the steam from steeped eucalyptus leaves, is the best remedy we know.

Insomnia.—The next time a sufferer finds himself awake, say 2 or 3 o'clock in the morning, instead of merely trying to banish the painful thought and repeating numbers, according to habit, let him revert at once to the dream which was the cause of his awakening, and try to go on with it. Sleep will come soon. It is stated on good authority that this experiment, oft repeated, has never been known to fail.

A correspondent of the *Lancet* gives the following method of self-asphyxiation as an effectual remedy for insomnia in his own case: After taking a deep inspiration, he holds his breath till discomfort is felt, then repeats the process a second and third time. As a rule this is enough to procure sleep. A slight degree of asphyxia is thus relied on as a soporific agent.

Leprosy.—An interesting report by the Hawaiian Board of Health is in our hands; incomplete statistics give the number of lepers in the several islands of the Hawaiian group on January 1, 1888, as 400. A statement of the leper population at Leper Settlement at Molokai for the biennial period ending March 31, 1888, is 749.

The report says: "Accurate statistics as to the number of lepers still at large in the various communities of this country cannot be obtained." It is estimated from the best data obtainable, that there were 644 lepers at large on the islands on March 31, 1888.

The report says: "The rations furnished each leper at the Leper Settlement on Molokai are abundant for the support of any adult Hawaiian."

One of the embarrassing questions the board is called upon to decide is, how many of the non-leper friends and relatives of the afflicted ones shall be allowed to go and live with them at the leper settlement as helpers, or *kokuas*, the number of applicants being in excess of the demand. The great obstacle to be overcome in carrying out the law of segregation consists in the fact that the Hawaiians do not appreciate and refuse to be convinced that leprosy is a communicable disease. It is with them as if devotion to a fatal sentimentality had bid defiance to every instinct of self-preservation. Marriages between leprous and non-leprous individuals are freely contracted, and the intimacies are not prevented by the fact of potent evidences of the disease. "If this race is ever to be rescued from the slough into which it is sinking, the fatal lethargy that stupefies them must be dispelled, the instinct of self-preservation must be awakened, and it must be written upon their hearts, as with the point of a diamond, that to voluntarily contaminate one's self with leprosy is a crime. In spite of a number of claims to the contrary, we believe it safe to say that no one has been able to prove, to the satisfaction of the medical profession, who very rightly demand full proof in such cases, that a single unmistakable case of this disease has been definitely cured." Says the report: "It is necessary always to bear in mind that the symptoms of leprosy, like those of some other diseases, have a way of receding or entirely disappearing for a time, only to show themselves again when least expected."

Government physicians generally attribute the causes which are checking the increase of the Hawaiian population to be leprosy; also the indolent and easy nature of the natives, which causes them to rest content, provided they can obtain the bare necessities of life. They are content to sit idle while their places are being filled with Chinese, and their lands are gradually passing from their possession. This apathy causes them to degenerate, both mentally and physically, and thus leads to the smallness of families and the general extinction of the race.

The following description of how this terrible disease develops and affects the patient is taken from the Hankow (China) Medical Mission report: "Leprosy is common. It chiefly affects men who work in the field; we have met with it in brothers; it is occasionally met with in women. The age varies from ten to fifty years. Often the first symptom complained of is some localized anæsthesia—which is sometimes quite accidentally discovered—in the feet, hands, or face, which are the parts that are most commonly affected. The sensory nerves are first affected, and sensation as a rule absent partially or completely. The anæsthesia is followed by want of free use of affected parts; the circulation is also impaired in those parts; the hair on the eyebrows falls out. A peculiar punched-out-looking ulcer, with a very fetid discharge, is often met in the feet; sometimes, but not so often, in the hands. As the disease advances, which it does very slowly—it often apparently remains stationary for years—the face broadens, becomes square, glazed, irregular and nodular; nodules are also found in the mucous membrane of the lips and in the nerves; perspiration is absent; the natural expression of the face is completely changed; the patient looks old and sad. As the disease further advances, the toes and fingers drop off, and by and by part of the limb. The general health is never affected. Treatment is not very satisfactory; symptoms seem to be controlled for a time, but never cured."

Lockjaw.—Professor Renzi, of Naples, records several cases of tetanus successfully treated by absolute rest. The method advocated is as follows: The patient's ears are closed with wax, after which he is placed in a perfectly dark room, far from any noise. He is made to understand that safety lies in perfect rest. The room is carpeted heavily in order to relieve the noise of stepping about. The nurse enters every quarter of an hour with a well-shaded lantern, using more the sense of touch than sight to find the bed. Liquid food (milk, eggs in beef tea, and water) is carefully given, so that mastication is not necessary. Constipation is not interfered with. Mild doses of belladonna or secale are given to relieve pain. This treatment does not shorten the disease, but under it the paroxysms grow milder, and finally cease. Numerous physicians attest to the value of this treatment.

Marriage.—The *Medical Record* says the unpopularity of marriage in England continues unabated, and last year was the first in recent times in which, while the price of wheat fell, the marriage rate remained stationary. It is now 14.2 per 1,000. The decline in the popularity of matrimony is greatest with those who have already had some experience of wedded life. Between 1876 and 1888 the marriage rate fell 12 per cent for bachelors and spinsters, 27 per cent for widowers, 31 per cent for widows.

Another interesting fact is that the births have now reached the lowest rate recorded since civil registration began. In 1876 the rate was 36.3 per 1,000; it is now 30.6. This is very satisfactory, and it is also notable that the illegitimate birth-rate has declined, the proportion, 4.6 per cent, being the lowest yet registered. The worst feature in the Registrar-General's returns, however, is the fact that the male births had fallen in proportion to the female; in the last ten years 1,038 boys were born for every 1,000 girls, and last year the male preponderance had dropped by 5, and is now standing at 1,033 to 1,000.

M. Huth has recently published a valuable book on consanguinity. There is no lack of instances of enforced consanguinity, in the matter of marriage, in isolated communities, according to M. Huth, to disprove the assumption that physical degeneration is likely to result from the practice. An investigation into a number of unions between uncles and nieces, nephews and aunts, and cousins in the first and second degree, gives an average of children rather above than below the general average, though this is attributed to some extent to the comparatively early age at which such unions are generally contracted. Breeders inform us that the results are markedly in favor of consanguineous unions between healthy, well-bred animals. Unions between men or animals of widely different varieties, on the other hand, have a decidedly injurious effect on the off-spring, and beyond a certain limit are almost absolutely sterile. Mulattoes and the half-breeds of India and America are striking examples of the deterioration to which such racial disparity gives rise. The great point to bear in mind is that the union of individuals with the same morbid tendencies intensifies the taint, and that, too, quite irrespective of any consanguinity. The moral, according to the author, is that the reasons which have led to the prohibition of marriages within certain degrees of relationship are social, and not physiological.

Malaria (Chills and Fever).—Mr. W. S. Green, editor of the *Weekly Colusa Sun*, of this State, has made careful investigations on the malaria question. We quote from his issue of May 12, 1888:—

"*Irrigation and Malaria.*—At the irrigation convention held at Riverside in March, '84, a paper by W. S. Green was read on the subject of 'Irrigation on Health.' The writer took a new departure, and combated notions held for ages; that is, he held that however much the received notions of malaria might hold good as to other climates, they were not correct when applied to California, where the air was in motion pretty much all the while. Mr. Green received the highest indorsement of his ideas, and they have come to be accepted as correct. His statement of facts has been verified by almost all observing men.

"*To the Pres. of the Irrigation Convention, Riverside, Cal.*—

"Having taken great interest in the problem of irrigation for twenty years and over, I had intended to be present at your meeting, but at this date I find it will be impossible. If a man possesses a mite of knowledge or an idea on this great subject, it is his duty to give his co-workers the benefit of it.

"During a residence of thirty-four years in the Sacramento Valley, I have had time and opportunity to observe and to study its sanitary conditions, and these observations bear directly, I think, on the subject of the effect of irrigation on the health of a country. I am led by these observations to reject almost *in toto* the long-accepted theory of infection by malaria from the atmosphere, that is, so far as it pertains to California. I will not consume your time with a technical dissertation, but will state some facts as briefly as possible, and in plain, homely phrase.

"When I saw people living all along the margins of the tules, where in summer the water became hot and stale and full of decaying vegetation, and hundreds of forms of animal life, and yet remain entirely free from malarial influence, I began to think there was some mistake in the accepted theory. I do not pretend to say that all the people living along the tule margins were or are healthy. All who occupy some places seem to be attacked by chills, while the occupants of places close by are never so attacked. Health is the rule. I saw that all these people, those on the healthy and those on the sickly places, must breathe the same air, coming to them from the same hot, stagnant water and decaying vegetation, and I concluded that malaria was not in the air. But I investigated further.

"There are clay, or, as some call them, hardpan banks to the upper Sacramento River, which are from a quarter of a mile to a mile apart. The river, for some very indefinite number of centuries, has vibrated between these banks—washing in on one side and filling in on the other. There is, then, an old or clay formation and a newer or alluvial formation; of course, there is alluvium on top of the clay, but this is not to our purpose. When I first saw the valley in 1850, this new land, some of it as high as the old, was covered with pea vines, blackberry vines, and a dense undergrowth generally, while the other grew wild oats and was usually as open as our wheat-fields. I began to notice that those people who built their houses and *dug their wells* on a newer formation generally had chills, while the others, as a rule, had not. Sometimes these sickly and healthy places would be but a few feet apart. They breathed the same air, but they *did not drink the same water*. I began to conclude that these people, both along the river and around the margins of the tules, drank the germ of disease and did not breathe it, and I continued my observations.

"The town of Colusa is built upon the old, or clay formation, and the people are entirely free from the so-called malarial influence. They are almost entirely free from chills, typhoid fevers, diphtheria, etc., but just at the lower end of the town there is evidence that the river at one time ran almost at right angles with its present course, and while the land is just as high, and very large oaks grew upon it, showing the formation to be very old—the span of human life taken as a measure—yet in digging and boring wells, as well as by the indigenous growth, the very great difference in the age of the formation was apparent. Upon this new formation an extension to the town was located, and among other buildings the county hospital was placed there. The patients and employes of the hospital all had chills for several years, until the physician-in-charge, Dr. W. H. Belton, noticed that the people generally who used water from wells on this newly-made land had chills, while the others had not, and caused pipes from the town waterworks, into which river water was pumped, to be laid to the hospital. There was an *immediate* change. At the commencement of the use of river water, there were some forty persons in the hospital, all with chills, but since the building has been almost entirely free from it. There could be no more conclusive evidence that these people *drank* the germ of the disease and *did not breathe it*.

"It is claimed that after a wet season there is more malaria in the air, and that hence people are more subject to disease. I have investigated this, and my observations, extended over a number of years, have convinced me that the water in the wells is simply raised to a newer stratum, one not thoroughly washed, as it were, and that people drink the germ of disease, and do not breathe it.

"My conclusions are, therefore, that irrigation will tend to bring on malarial disorders, as it raises the water in wells to a newer stratum of earth, but no further. When we irrigate so as to produce this effect we must *go down* after pure drinking water, or bring it to our houses in pipes. The effect of disorders thus brought about is easily remedied.

"I do not wish to be understood as maintaining that there may be no such thing as poison in the atmosphere. In some localities, where the air is not in motion every day, as it is here, the air, like standing water, may become stagnant. I know of some hotels in this valley totally void of drainage, and where the accumulated filth of a quarter of a century stands in the yards in cess-pools. In some countries this would kill ninety out of a hundred people who would stop in them a week, but here we feel no inconvenience from it, except in so far that the water may become impregnated. Air in motion, like water in motion, purifies itself, and hence I have come to the rejection of the theory of malaria in the air."

Of our own remedies we feel very proud because they are sure to kill chills and fever. There are two:—

First: Take the proportions of one (1) of sulphur to two (2) of gin, or 4 fluidounces of gin to 2 of sulphur. Let it stand overnight. For an adult take one teaspoonful of this mixture in a little water from 15 to 30 minutes before the attack. Remain in bed in a room warmed to 90° Fahr., for from 6 to 10 hours. This has not been known to fail.

Second: This requires much care and judgment. Take a whole nutmeg finely grated, and its equal quantity of pulverized alum, thoroughly mix them, and take at one dose; the *time* to take it has everything to do with its effect. It must be taken between 10 and 17 minutes before the shake is due to come on. Go to bed immediately, using double the usual amount of bedclothes, remain there from 1-1/2 to 3 hours, and both chills and fever will permanently depart. If the medicine is taken too soon (say 30 minutes before the shake), the attack will be more severe; if taken immediately after the shake it will increase the fever; in either case the dose will have to be repeated to effect a cure. This latter treatment completely cured the author.

Nervousness and Worry.—One meets few unworried people. Most faces bear lines of care. Men go anxious to their day's duties, rush through the hours with feverish speed, and bring hot brain and tumultuous pulse home at night for restless, unrefreshing sleep. This is not only a most unsatisfactory, but is also a most costly, mode of living. The other night the train lost two hours in running less than a hundred miles. "We have a hot box," was the polite conductor's reply to some impatient passengers who begged to know the cause of the long delays at stations. This hot-box trouble is not altogether unknown in human life. There are many people who move swiftly enough and with sufficient energy, but who grow feverish and are thus impeded in their progress. A great many failures in life must be charged to worrying. When a man worries he is impeded in several ways. For one thing he loses his head. He cannot think clearly. His brain is feverish, and will not act at its best. His mind becomes confused, and his decisions are not to be depended upon. The result is that a worried man never does his work as well as he should do it, or as he could do it if he were free from worry. He is apt to make mistakes. Marks of feverishness are sure to be seen somewhere in whatever he does. Remedy: Keep cool, think three times before you act once.

Obesity and Thinness.—To increase the weight; Eat, to the extent of satisfying a natural appetite, of fat meats, butter, cream, milk, cocoa, chocolate, bread, potatoes, peas, parsnips, carrots, beets, farinaceous food, or Indian corn, rice, tapioca, sago, corn-starch, pastry, custards, oatmeal, sugar, sweet wines, and ale. Avoid acids. Exercise as little as possible, sleep all you can, and don't worry or fret. To reduce the weight: Eat, to the extent of satisfying a natural appetite, of lean meat, poultry, game, eggs, milk moderately, green vegetables, turnips, succulent fruits, tea or coffee. Drink lime juice, lemonade, and acid drinks. Avoid fat, butter, cream, sugar, pastry, rice, sago, tapioca, corn-starch, potatoes, carrots, beets, parsnips, and sweet wines. Exercise freely.

Piles.—When piles become painful, whether they protrude or not, the patient should take a warm hip-bath and remain in until the pain ceases, extra precaution being taken for cleanliness, using pure white castile soap with the hip-bath. A careful diet of farinaceous and other easily-digested food, and regularity in going to stool, will suffice to cure the majority of cases. If the piles are bleeding, apply a salve of opium and nut-gall; if itching, a drop of oil of cade will give relief. Linseed oil, applied to the piles, is said to be an effective remedy. In severe cases of piles great relief is afforded by the use of suppositories made after the following formula: 2 grains sulphate morphina, 2 grains extract belladonna, 1 scruple tannin.

The above mixed with a sufficient quantity of cocoa butter to make twelve suppositories of one-half ounce each; one to be used every night on retiring.

Poisons.—Poisons may be classified under two distinct heads—*mineral* and *vegetable*. *Mineral poisons* are irritating and corrosive in their action. They produce a metallic taste in the mouth, burning pains in the throat, stomach, and bowels, and, often, violent retching and bloody vomiting, purging, cramps, cold sweats, and great depression. *Vegetable poisons* are chiefly narcotics, and many of them are as virulent as any in the mineral kingdom. They cause giddiness, drowsiness, stupor, insensibility or delirium, and oppressed breathing.

General Directions.—First and instantly dilute the poison with large draughts of warm water, either clear, or, if the particular poison is known, containing the proper antidote. This will usually cause vomiting, which is to be desired. If vomiting does not soon occur, excite it. Protect as much as possible the lining membrane of the stomach and bowels from contact with the poison by large and frequent doses of sweet-oil, mucilage of gum arabic, flaxseed tea, milk, etc. Melted cosmoline, vaseline, butter, or lard will serve for this purpose. Keep up the temperature by means of warm blankets, hot bottles, etc.; and if there are marked evidences of sinking, such as a failure of the pulse, or very feeble, gasping respiration, give a little stimulus, preferably by injection into the bowels. In the case of an adult, a tablespoonful of brandy, whisky or gin, with an equal quantity of water, may be administered in this manner every five or ten minutes, until reaction sets in—that is, until the face regains its color, the pulse becomes stronger, and the breathing natural.

A general antidote for all cases of poisoning, where the nature of the poison is unknown, is a mixture of carbonate of magnesia, powdered charcoal, and hydrated sesquioxide of iron, equal parts, in water.

POISONS—MINERAL. *Acids.*—*Muriatic* (spirit of salt), *nitric* (aqua fortis), *sulphuric* (oil of vitriol), *oxalic, nitro-muriatic,* etc. Nitric and sulphuric acids are sometimes used for the removal of warts; oxalic acid is often employed for taking out iron or ink stains; muriatic and nitro-muriatic acids are frequently prescribed medicinally. As soon as a poisonous dose has been swallowed, seek for something which will neutralize the acid. Powdered chalk, whiting, magnesia, or lime scraped from a wall and stirred in water, may be given in any of these cases. For sulphuric or muriatic acid also administer soap-suds, sweet milk, common soap cut into small pieces, baking or washing soda, or saleratus, giving these latter in very small quantities at a time, so as not to produce dangerous distension of the stomach, from the evolution of gas. In the case of sulphuric acid, water must not be used freely at first, at least not unless it contains some antidote, as the heat produced, when this acid and water are mixed, is sufficient of itself to cause serious damage.

Ammonia, and other alkalies (Caustic Potash, Soda or Lime).—Antidotes: Vinegar, lemon juice, or a weak solution of tartaric acid, to be followed immediately with sweet-oil or mucilage of gum arabic, and an emetic. Also give an injection of boiled starch. Pain may be relieved with laudanum, in doses of ten to fifteen drops, as the paroxysms occur.

Antimony (Butter of Antimony, Tartar Emetic).—Encourage vomiting. The antidotes are milk, tea, tannic acid.

Arsenic, Ratsbane, Paris Green, Cobalt, and all arsenical preparations used as rat poisons.—Give the whites of five or six eggs, beaten in half a pint of water; or, flour and water, barley water, flaxseed tea, or magnesia. Also administer an emetic of five grains of sulphate of copper (blue vitriol), or fifteen grains of sulphate of zinc (white vitriol), ipecac, or mustard and water. After the vomiting, give hydrated sesquioxide of iron in tablespoon doses, every fifteen minutes, until danger is past. This is the best-known antidote for arsenic, and should be procured fresh from the drug store if possible.

Chloral, Chloroform, Ether.—Cold water should be sprinkled over the face and applied to the head. If breathing is suspended, treat the patient for artificial respiration. The use of electricity is recommended.

Corrosive Sublimate (Bedbug Poison), *Calomel* (Mercury).—The whites of three or four eggs, beaten in water, should be given without delay. If eggs are not at hand, flour or thin starch gruel, mucilage of gum arabic, or milk, will answer. An emetic should be taken immediately after the antidote has been administered.

Iodine (used for external application).—If it has been swallowed, give a paste of starch, or flour and water.

Lead, Salts of (Sugar of Lead, Lead Paint).—After an emetic, administer as much Epsom salt, or Glauber's salt, as the patient can drink. Then give large quantities of milk and whites of eggs.

Lunar Caustic, Nitrate of Silver.—Give a large teaspoonful of common salt, in a glass of water. Repeat the dose every ten minutes for an hour. Then give a dose of castor-oil, and let the patient drink freely of flaxseed tea, barley water, or sweet milk.

Muriates of Tin and Zinc.—These poisons are sometimes found in canned goods—fruits, vegetables, fish, and meats. They cause nausea, vomiting, sudden failure of the vital forces, and sometimes cramps and convulsions. Milk, the whites of eggs, strong tea, or tincture of Peruvian bark, should be given. After the violent symptoms have subsided, the patient should drink freely of flaxseed tea or barley water.

Phosphorus, Matches.—Give large quantities of warm water containing calcined magnesia, chalk, or whiting.

Prussic Acid.—Liquor of ammonia, in doses of ten drops to a tablespoonful of water, should be given every fifteen minutes, until the patient is out of danger. Also apply smelling salts to the nose, dash cold water in the face, and give stimulants.

Verdigris.—Give sugar, milk, and whites of eggs in large quantities, then strong tea, but no acids of any kind.

POISONS—VEGETABLE. *Aconite.*—Induce free vomiting, then give brandy or whisky every half hour until the dangerous symptoms are allayed.

Alcohol, Spirits.—Give half a teaspoonful of aromatic spirits of ammonia in sweetened water every half hour. Bromide of potassa, in doses of fifteen to thirty grains, every two or three hours, will also be found useful.

Cocaine is the alkaloid of the coca plant of South American origin. It is generally employed in the form of muriate of cocaine and principally used as a local anæsthetic. It should only be used under the direction of a physician. It may occasion dangerous effects even in doses usually deemed safe. When it has been taken internally, the proper antidote is a powerful emetic followed by stimulants—such as liquor and spirits of ammonia—administered internally. When it has been used to a dangerous extent externally, give whisky or brandy and ammonia.

Laudanum, Opium, Paregoric, Morphia, Belladonna, Hyoscyamus, Stramonium, and Conium.—An emetic of mustard and water, twenty grains of sulphate of zinc (white vitriol), or thirty grains of powdered ipecac, should be given. Strong coffee, brandy, or whisky should then be administered in large quantities, and the patient walked around the room. Slapping, pinching, dashing cold water in the face, and even whipping, may be necessary to keep the patient awake.

Strychnine (Nux Vomica).—Give an emetic of a solution of sulphate of zinc (white vitriol), or a strong infusion of tobacco; or inject into the bowels bromide of potassium, thirty grains, and the extract of coca, one-half ounce. During the spasms, the patient should breathe chloroform or ether from a saturated cloth held to the nose and mouth.

Toadstools (False Mushrooms) and other poisonous plants and seeds, such as are liable to be picked up and eaten by children.—Empty the stomach at once by an emetic you have at hand.

Coffee poisoning occurs mostly with well-to-do people—those who are overfed. Tea poisoning comes to hard-working, half-starved women. The symptoms of coffee poisoning are want of appetite, sleeplessness, and nervous tremblings, with various indications of indigestion and torpor of liver. Tea poisoning requires rest and nourishment; but the victim of coffee excess usually needs to unload his system by exercise on a low diet.

Antipyrine.—Dr. T. E. Smith, of Cincinnati, had his whole right side paralyzed by a ten-grain dose of antipyrine. The dose is an ordinary one. This powerful drug is much resorted to by grippe victims.

Removal of Foreign Substances.—Considering the frequency with which foreign bodies are swallowed, especially by children, the best treatment to employ in such cases should be generally known. A variety of such methods have been advocated, but just now the so-called "potato cure" appears to be the most popular. One physician not long ago reported that he had successfully applied it with the best results in three cases. One was that of a 6-year-old boy, who swallowed a small weight; another that of a girl, 9 years old, who had swallowed a nail; and the remaining one that of a woman who had swallowed a set of teeth. He fed the patients for three days on nothing but potatoes. This treatment is a method in vogue among the pickpockets of London, who, swallowing their booty, live on potatoes until the stolen articles have passed down and out of the body.

Rheumatism.—Those who have a tendency to that disease should "take a stitch" now and free their systems from all injurious retained matter. They should live abstemiously, exercise freely, keep the skin active by frequent bathing, the bowels open with fruits, and drink water in large quantities. Water dissolves and washes waste matter out of the system; it is therefore an absolute essential where there is any impairment in the action of the kidneys, bowels, or skin. He who applies this simple treatment, and takes proper care of himself otherwise, may feel quite secure from attacks of rheumatism.

"Practical Medicine" suggests: "Make a concentrated emulsion of black soap, 200 grammes; add thereto 100 or 150 grammes of turpentine, and shake the whole vigorously until a beautiful creamy emulsion is obtained. For a bath take half of this mixture, which possesses an agreeable pine odor.

After remaining in the bath a quarter of an hour, the patient should get into bed, when a prickling sensation, not disagreeable, however, is felt over the entire body; then, after a nap, he awakens with marked diminution of rheumatic pains."

Flour of sulphur dusted into the soles of the shoes and stockings is said to be a perfect preventive. The exciting causes of rheumatism are cold or wet applied to the body when in a state of heat, exposure to cold winds, remaining long in wet clothes, sleeping in a damp bed, or blood-poisoning. Acute attacks of rheumatism should be treated by painting the affected part with tincture of iodine.

Seasickness.—Experts claim that seasickness can be regulated by a system of breathing. One must sit still and time the breathing to the upward and downward motion of the boat. As the boat falls there should be a full expiration, and as the boat rises start on an inspiration ending just as the boat begins to drop.

Sleep.—The "Home Maker" says: "Up to the fifteenth year most young people require ten hours, and till the twentieth year, nine hours. After that age everyone finds out how much he or she requires, though, as a general rule, at least six to eight hours are necessary. Eight hours' sleep will prevent more nervous derangements in women than any medicine can cure. During growth there must be ample sleep if the brain is to develop to its full extent, and the more nervous, excitable, or precocious a child is, the longer sleep should it get if its intellectual progress is not to come to a premature standstill, or its life be cut short at an early age."

A doctor of prominence says: "There is no doubt in my mind but the belief that human beings should sleep with their bodies lying north and south has its foundation in true scientific facts. Each human system has two magnetic poles—one positive and one negative. Now, it is true that some persons have the positive pole in the head and the negative pole in the feet, and *vice versa*. In order that the person sleeping should be in perfect harmony with the magnetic phenomena of the earth, the head, if it possesses the positive pole, should lie to the south, or if the feet possess the positive pole the head should lie to the north. The positive pole should always lie opposite to the magnetic center of the continent and thus maintain a magnetic equilibrium. The positive pole of the person draws one way, but the magnetic pole of the earth draws the other way and forces the blood toward the feet, affects the iron in the system, tones up the nerves, and makes sleep refreshing and invigorating. But if the person sleeps the wrong way and fails to become magnetically *en rapport* with the earth, he will then probably be too magnetic, and he will have a fever resulting from the magnetic forces working too fast, or he will not be magnetic enough, and the great strain will cause a feeling of lassitude, sleep will not be refreshing, and in the morning he will have no more energy than there is in a cake of soap. Some persons may scoff at these ideas, but the greatest scientific men of the world have studied the subject. Only recently the French Academy of Science made experiments upon the body of a guillotined man, which go to prove that each human system is in itself an electric battery, one electrode being represented by the head, the other by the feet. The body was taken immediately after death and placed on a pivot, to move as it might. After some vacillation the head portion turned toward the north, the body then remaining stationary. One of the professors turned it half way around, but it soon regained its original position, and the same result was repeatedly obtained, until organic movement finally ceased."

Small-pox and Vaccination.—Notwithstanding existing prejudices, statistics prove the great usefulness of vaccination. In small-pox epidemics, of those persons attacked who have not been vaccinated, one case in four is fatal; while of those who have been vaccinated, the death rate is not one in four hundred and fifty. In cities, it is important that every infant should be vaccinated before it is six months old. In the country, the operation may be deferred until the infant is a year old. Care should be taken to have the virus fresh and from the cow. The taking of virus from a child, or an adult, should never be allowed, as constitutional diseases are often transmitted in that way. Vaccination is performed by making a small incision in the skin and introducing the virus on the point of a lancet or needle. On the third day, if the desired result has been attained, a small red spot may be seen. This increases in size, becomes elevated, and, by the sixth day, is filled with a clear, yellow liquid. About the eighth day, the pustule is fully formed, when symptoms of small-pox are usually felt,—headache, shivering, loss of appetite, etc. These symptoms subside in a day or two; the fluid in the pustule dries up, and a scab forms, which remains about two weeks and then disappears, leaving a scar. The affected part should be protected by a loose bandage, and all scratching or rubbing prevented.

The theory in regard to vaccination is that the disease in a mild form takes hold of the system, and either completely or partially destroys the liability to contract the same disease in the future. If the destruction is only partial, it can be made total by future vaccinations. All authorities agree that it is necessary to revaccinate frequently—just as often, in fact, as the system shows itself in readiness to take the vaccinations. Then as often as once in five or seven years vaccination should be repeated in order to obtain complete immunity from small-pox.

Superstitions.—Numerous are the dangerous superstitions about marriage. For instance, the bride must not try on her wedding gown, or ill-luck will follow. She must not look in the glass after she is fully dressed and ready for the ceremony. She must not enter her new home by stepping over the threshold, but must be carried over it by one of her relatives. A piece of the bride's cake must be broken over her head as soon as she is safely on the other side. It is very unlucky for her to be in a happy state on her wedding-day. She must be as dolorous as possible, violent fits of weeping being especially beneficial.

It is a good idea for the brides-maids to throw away as many pins as possible on the wedding-day, as this will hasten marriage. The bride should throw away her slipper in leaving the wedding feast, and she who catches it will be the first married. The month of May is generally conceded to be the most unfortunate for marriages. The lucky months are January, April, August, October, and November. January is especially lucky.

Lovers should carefully avoid passing a sharp or pointed instrument from one to the other. Such things tend to cause quarrels. The wedding should be put off by all means if a cat sneezes on the eve of the wedding-day. It should never take place if the cat is black. To sweep dust over a girl's feet or legs will be certain to make an old maid of her.

Should the younger sister of a family marry first, the older sisters will be condemned to lasting celibacy unless they dance at her wedding in their stocking-feet.

The wedding-ring of the mother is an infallible cure for eruptions on the skin of the child. The ring must be rubbed three times around each sore. Cure is certain.

The virtue of the dew that glitters and sparkles in every leaf and flower of a May morning has been recognized from the earliest times. If a young girl wishes to obtain and preserve a glorious complexion she should venture out of a May morning and wash her face in this dew.

To spit in the hand before undertaking anything, whether in love, war, or business, will not fail to bring luck. If you are out fishing, do not step over your rod, or you will catch no more fish than did Simple Simon in his mother's pail.

Of births, it may be said in general that a crying child will grow up to be a great and useful man. This omen is not very clearly settled, however, and is often given the other way. Some seer far back in the ages discovered the following: Born on Monday, fair in the face; born on Tuesday, full of God's grace; born on Wednesday, sour and sad; born on Thursday, merry and glad; born on Friday, worthily given; born on Saturday, work for your living; born on Sunday, you will never know want.

To recall a person after they have left the house is bad luck. To go back for something forgotten is also bad luck, unless you sit down before going out again.

If, when you sit before the fire, a live coal jumps out, it is a sign that you are to have good luck, especially in money matters. To wash in water another has washed in is not only bad sanitarily, but also superstitiously. He who makes many crumbs at the table will never have any money to spare. It is flying in the face of fortune to sweep dust out of the front door or to allow it to be swept out. In so doing you are sweeping out your good luck. To count one's gains brings luck, but to find money is the worst possible luck.

The 4-leaved clover once found, should be treasured, as every school-child knows and believes. It brings luck of every description. Eve attempted to carry a 4-leaved shamrock of precious stone from Paradise with her, but it fell and shattered at her feet. Think of the disaster thus entailed upon the human race!

To see the moon over the left shoulder is as unlucky as to hold the four of clubs at cards. But the new moon seen over the right shoulder, or straight in front, portends fortune as smiling as her own bright rays.

www.ingramcontent.com/pod-product-compliance
Lightning Source LLC
Chambersburg PA
CBHW081114080526
44587CB00021B/3591